Bouquet of BLOOMS

15 Quilts, Wall Hangings, and Pillows

LEISURE ARTS, INC.
Little Rock, Arkansas

Table

OF CONTENTS

EDITORIAL STAFF
Editor-in-Chief: Susan White Sullivan
Quilt Publications Director: Cheryl Johnson
Special Projects Director:
  Susan Frantz Wiles
Senior Prepress Director: Mark Hawkins
Art Publications Director: Rhonda Shelby
Technical Editor: Lisa Lancaster
Associate Editor: Jean Lewis
Editorial Writer: Susan McManus Johnson
Art Category Manager: Lora Puls
Graphic Artist: Jacob Casleton
Imaging Technician: Stephanie Johnson
Prepress Technician: Janie Marie Wright
Photography Manager: Katherine Laughlin
Contributing Photographer: Ken West
Contributing Photostylist: Sondra Daniel
Publishing Systems Administrator:
  Becky Riddle
Mac Information Technology Specialist:
  Robert Young

BUSINESS STAFF
President and Chief Executive Officer:
  Rick Barton
**Vice President and Chief Operations
Officer:** Tom Siebenmorgen
Vice President of Sales: Mike Behar
Director of Finance and Administration:
  Laticia Mull Dittrich
National Sales Director: Martha Adams
Creative Services: Chaska Lucas
Information Technology Director:
  Hermine Linz
Controller: Francis Caple
Vice President, Operations: Jim Dittrich
Retail Customer Service Manager:
  Stan Raynor
Print Production Manager: Fred F. Pruss

Library of Congress Control Number:
2011927781
ISBN-13: 978-1-60900-242-8

FLOWERS NEVER GO OUT OF STYLE, AND THE SAME IS TRUE OF FLORAL QUILTS. THESE CLASSIC LEISURE ARTS QUILTS ARE ALL ABOUT CAPTURING THE BEAUTY OF FLOWERS. WHETHER YOU CHOOSE TO USE FLORAL PRINTS OR CREATE YOUR FLOWERS WITH APPLIQUÉ OR FOUNDATION PIECING, THERE ARE BLOOMS HERE THAT WILL FIT THE MODERN HOME. NOW AS EVER, QUILTS ARE ALSO THE MOST THOUGHTFUL OF GIFTS. MAKE A FLOWER BASKET WALL HANGING FOR A NEW HOMEOWNER. CREATE AN ELEGANT BABY QUILT FOR A NEW MOM. OR SIMPLY FASHION A FEW PILLOWS TO BRIGHTEN YOUR OWN CORNER OF THE WORLD. LET THESE VINTAGE DESIGNS INSPIRE YOU TO GROW A WHOLE NEW GARDEN OF CREATIVE QUILTS!

Tulip QUILT

Finished Quilt Size:
79" x 88" (201 cm x 224 cm)

Finished Block Size:
9" x 9" (23 cm x 23 cm)

Yardage Requirements

Yardage is based on 43"/44" (109 cm x 112 cm) wide fabric with a usable width of 40" (102 cm).

- 6 yds (5.5 m) of white solid fabric
- $3^3/_4$ yds (3.4 m) of pink solid fabric
- $1^1/_4$ yds (1.1 m) of green solid fabric
- $7^1/_4$ yds (6.6 m) of fabric for backing
- $5/_8$ yd (57 cm) of fabric for binding

You will also need:
- 87" x 96" (221 cm x 244 cm) rectangle of batting

Cutting the Pieces

*Follow **Template Cutting**, page 81, to make template from triangle pattern, page 7. Follow **Rotary Cutting**, page 80, to cut fabric. Cut all strips across the selvage-to-selvage width of the fabric unless otherwise indicated. Borders are cut longer than necessary and will be trimmed to fit quilt top center. All measurements include $1/_4$" seam allowances.*

From white solid fabric:
- Cut 9 strips $1^5/_8$" wide. From these strips, cut 216 **small squares** $1^5/_8$" x $1^5/_8$".
- Cut 16 strips $2^3/_4$" wide. From these strips, cut 216 **medium squares** $2^3/_4$" x $2^3/_4$".
- Use template to cut 144 **triangles**; cut 144 triangles in reverse. Mark dots on fabric triangles.

From pink solid fabric:
- Cut 2 *lengthwise* **top/bottom borders** $3^1/_2$" x $82^1/_2$".
- Cut 2 *lengthwise* **side borders** $3^1/_2$" x $91^1/_2$".
- From remaining fabric width, cut 15 strips 5" wide. From these strips, cut 72 **large squares** 5" x 5".
- Use template to cut 72 **triangles**; cut 72 triangles in reverse. Mark dots on fabric triangles.

From green solid fabric:
- Cut 3 strips $1^5/_8$" wide. From these strips, cut 72 **small squares** $1^5/_8$" x $1^5/_8$".
- Use template to cut 72 **triangles**; cut 72 triangles in reverse. Mark dots on fabric triangles.

From fabric for binding:
- Cut 9 **binding strips** $2^1/_8$"w.

CHOOSE YOUR FAVORITE
ROSY SHADE TO CREATE
THIS TULIP QUILT,
OR USE A VARIETY OF
FLORAL PRINT SCRAPS.
EITHER WAY, YOUR
FINGERS WILL FLY
TO SEW THESE BIG
PATCHWORK PIECES!

Assembling the Quilt Top

*Follow **Machine Piecing**, page 81, and **Pressing**, page 83. Use a ¹/₄" seam allowance.*

1. Matching dots, sew 1 pink **triangle** and 1 white **triangle** together to make **Unit 1**. Make 72 Unit 1's. Sew 1 pink **triangle** and 1 white **triangle** together to make **Unit 2**. Make 72 Unit 2's.
2. Matching dots, sew 1 green **triangle** and 1 white **triangle** together to make **Unit 3**. Make 72 Unit 3's. Sew 1 green **triangle** and 1 white **triangle** together to make **Unit 4**. Make 72 Unit 4's.
3. Sew 3 white **small squares** and 1 green **small square** together to make **Unit 5**. Make 72 Unit 5's.
4. Sew 1 white **medium square**, 1 **Unit 1**, and 1 **Unit 5** together to make **Unit 6**. Make 72 Unit 6's.
5. Sew 1 **Unit 3**, 1 pink **large square**, and 1 **Unit 2** together to make **Unit 7**. Make 72 Unit 7's.
6. Sew 2 white **medium squares** and 1 **Unit 4** together to make **Unit 8**. Make 72 Unit 8's.
7. Sew **Units 6**, **7**, and **8** together to make **Block**. Make 72 Blocks.
8. Sew 8 **Blocks** together to make a **Row**. Make 9 Rows.
9. Sew 9 **Rows** together to make center section of **Quilt Top**.
10. Follow **Adding Mitered Borders**, page 86, to add borders to complete **Quilt Top**.

Completing the Quilt

1. Follow **Quilting**, page 87, to mark, layer, and quilt as desired. Our quilt is hand stitched with crosshatch quilting 1" apart across the center section of the quilt top and in diagonal lines ³/₈" apart along the borders.
2. Follow **Making Straight-Grain Binding**, page 92, and use **binding strips** to make binding. Follow **Attaching Binding with Mitered Corners**, page 92, to attach binding to quilt.

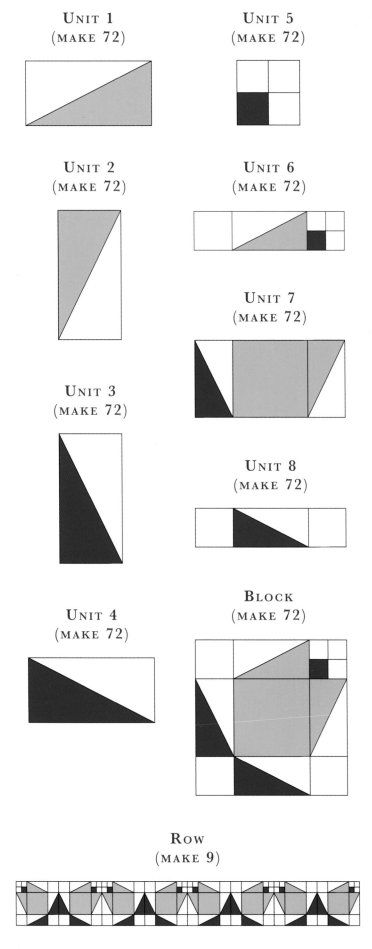

UNIT 1 (MAKE 72)

UNIT 2 (MAKE 72)

UNIT 3 (MAKE 72)

UNIT 4 (MAKE 72)

UNIT 5 (MAKE 72)

UNIT 6 (MAKE 72)

UNIT 7 (MAKE 72)

UNIT 8 (MAKE 72)

BLOCK (MAKE 72)

ROW (MAKE 9)

QUILT TOP DIAGRAM

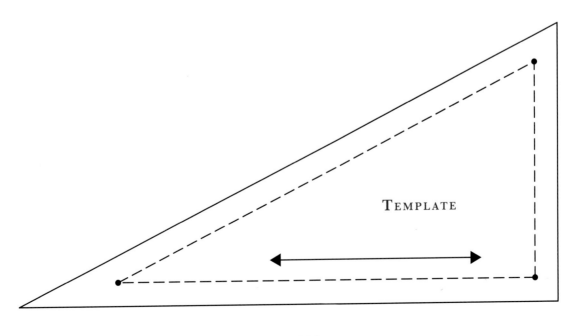

TEMPLATE

Dogwood
QUILT

FINISHED QUILT SIZE:
67" x 96" (170 CM x 244 CM)

Yardage Requirements

Yardage is based on 43"/44" (109 cm/112 cm) wide fabric with a usable width of 40" (102 cm).

$5^3/_4$ yds (5.3 m) of cream solid fabric
$1/_4$ yd (23 cm) of light pink solid fabric
$1/_2$ yd (46 cm) of pink solid fabric
$1/_4$ yd (23 cm) of dark pink solid fabric
$1/_4$ yd (23 cm) of yellow solid fabric
$3/_8$ yd (34 cm) of green solid fabric
$3/_8$ yd (34 cm) of brown solid fabric
$5^7/_8$ yds (5.4 m) of fabric for backing
$5/_8$ yd (57 m) of fabric for binding

You will also need:

75" x 104" (191 cm x 264 cm) piece of batting
Embroidery floss - pink, yellow, green, and brown

Pillow instructions given on page 14.

A LATTICE OF DOGWOOD BLOSSOMS BRINGS THE SWEETNESS OF
SPRINGTIME TO THIS BED QUILT. BLANKET STITCHES OUTLINE
EACH PIECE OF APPLIQUÉ, WHILE A TINY CRESCENT OF SATIN
STITCHES ADORNS EACH PETAL. THE EMBROIDERY ON THIS QUILT
WAS DONE BY HAND, BUT IF YOU DECIDE TO USE A MACHINE
BLANKET STITCH, YOU CAN GET SIMILAR RESULTS IN A FRACTION
OF THE TIME.

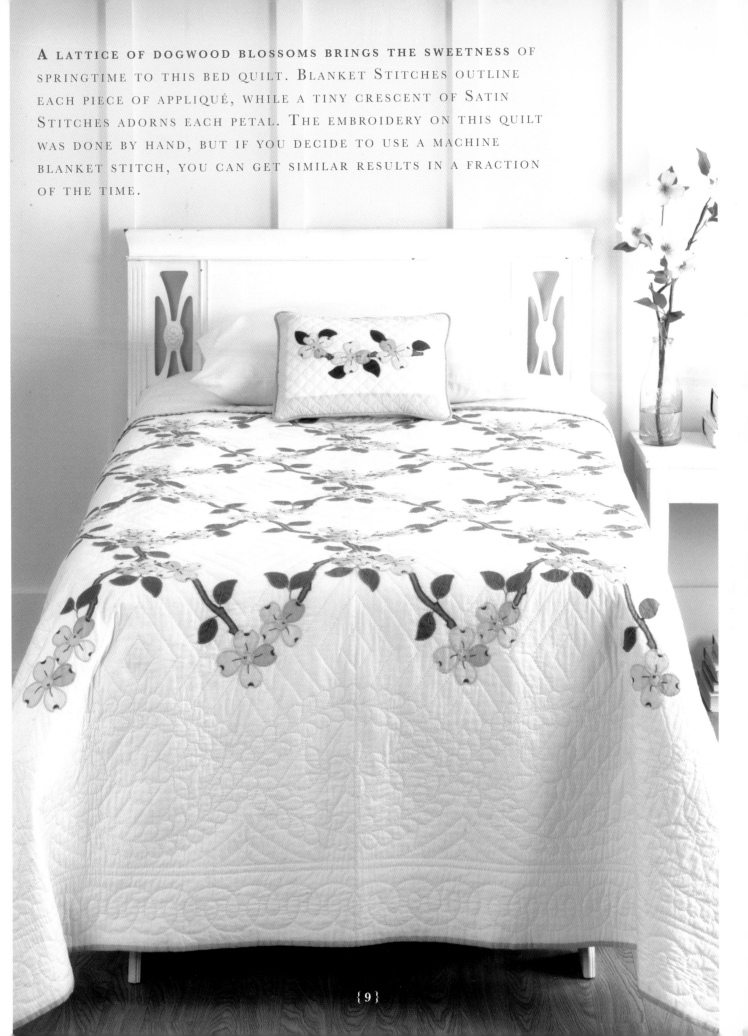

Cutting the Pieces

Follow Rotary Cutting, page 80, to cut fabric. Cut all strips across the selvage-to-selvage width of the fabric. All measurements include 1/4" seam allowances. Use patterns, pages 12-13, to cut appliqué pieces.

From cream solid fabric:
- Cut 2 **background pieces** 40" x 100".

From light pink solid fabric:
- Cut 25 **large flower petals**.
- Cut 36 **medium flower petals**.
- Cut 9 **small flower petals**.

From pink solid fabric:
- Cut 50 **large flower petals**.
- Cut 72 **medium flower petals**.
- Cut 18 **small flower petals**.

From dark pink solid fabric:
- Cut 25 **large flower petals**.
- Cut 36 **medium flower petals**.
- Cut 9 **small flower petals**.

From yellow solid fabric:
- Cut 70 **flower centers**.

From green solid fabric:
- Cut 126 **leaves** in any combination.

From brown solid fabric:
- Cut 9 *each* of all **branches**.

From fabric for binding:
- Cut 9 **binding strips** $2^1/8$"w.

Assembling the Quilt Top

Use a 1/4" seam allowance throughout. Use 3 strands of floss for all embroidery.

1. Referring to **Preparing the Backing**, page 88, use **background pieces** to assemble a 3-panel quilt top with 2 vertical seams. Centering vertical seams, trim background to $66^1/2$" x $95^1/2$". Fold quilt top into quarters; press to mark placement guidelines and center.
2. Refer to **Quilt Top Diagram** to pin appliqués in place.
3. Using brown floss for branches, pink floss for flowers, green floss for leaves, and yellow floss for centers, refer to **Hand Stitches**, page 96, to Blanket Stitch appliqués to background. Use brown floss to Stem Stitch detail lines in petals, Satin Stitch tips of petals, and Straight Stitch highlights in centers. Use green floss to Stem Stitch leaf stems and detail lines in leaves.

Completing the Quilt

1. Follow **Quilting**, page, 87, to mark, layer and quilt as desired. Our quilt is hand quilted.
2. Follow **Making Straight-Grain Binding**, page 92, and use **binding strips** to make binding. Follow **Attaching Binding with Mitered Corners**, page 92, to attach binding to quilt.

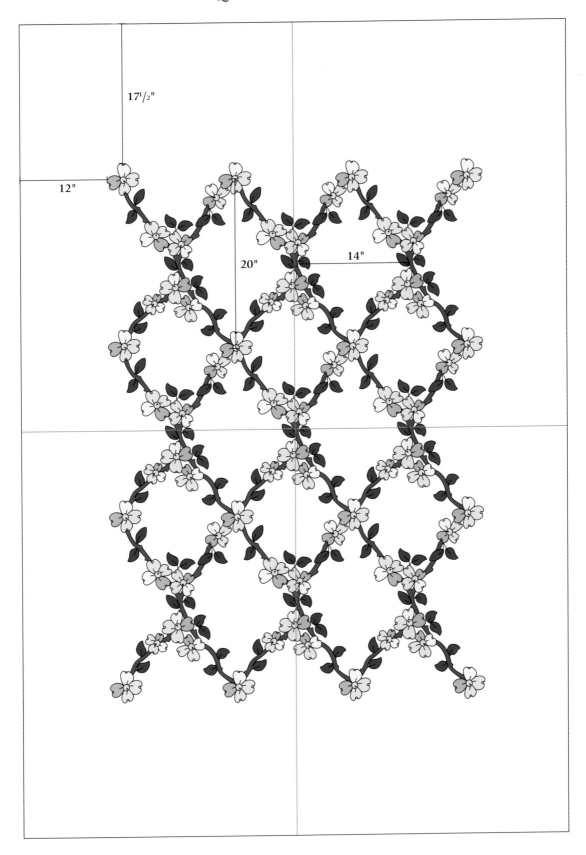

17$^{1}/_{2}$"

12"

20"

14"

LEAVES

SMALL FLOWER PETALS

LARGE FLOWER PETALS

MEDIUM FLOWER PETALS

FLOWER CENTER

BRANCHES

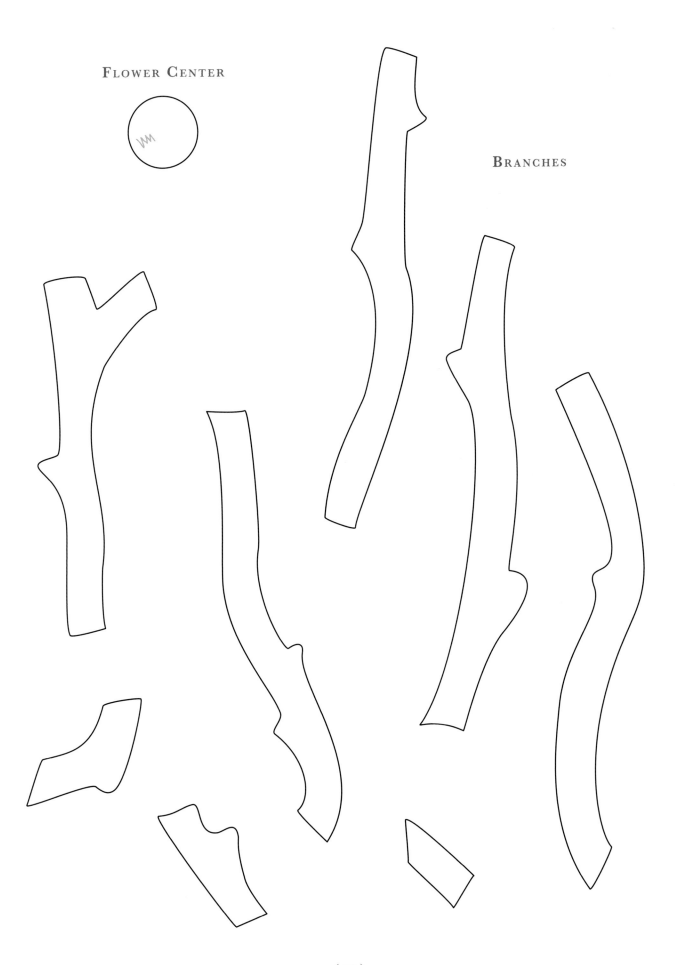

Dogwood
PILLOW

FINISHED PILLOW SIZE:
12" x 16" (30 CM x 41 CM)

Yardage Requirements

Yardage is based on 43"/44" (109 cm/112 cm) wide fabric with a usable width of 40" (102 cm).

  $1/2$ yd (46 cm) of cream solid fabric
  $1/8$ yd (11 cm) of light pink solid fabric
  $3/8$ yd (34 cm) of pink solid fabric
  $3/8$ yd (34 cm) of dark pink solid fabric
  $1/8$ yd (11 cm) of yellow solid fabric
  $1/8$ yd (11 cm) of green solid fabric
  $1/8$ yd (11 cm) of brown solid fabric

You will also need:

  16" x 20" (41 cm x 51 cm) piece of batting
  2 yds (1.8 m) of $1/4$" (6 mm) diameter cord
  Embroidery floss - pink, yellow, green,
   and brown
  Water-soluble fabric marking pen
  12" x 16" (30 cm x 41 cm) pillow form or
   fiberfill for stuffing

DOGWOOD BLOSSOMS ARE A BIT OF WOODLAND BEAUTY WE WOULD
ALL LOVE TO BRING INDOORS TO KEEP FOREVER—AND THIS PRETTY
PILLOW MAKES IT POSSIBLE. EASY EMBROIDERY SECURES THE
APPLIQUÉ PIECES WHILE ADDING DEFINITION.

Cutting the Pieces

*Follow **Rotary Cutting**, page 80, to cut fabric. Cut all strips across the selvage-to-selvage width of the fabric unless otherwise indicated. All measurements include ¹/₄" seam allowances. Use patterns, page 12 - 13 to cut appliqué pieces.*

From cream solid fabric:
- Cut **rectangle** 10" x 15" for top.
- Cut 2 rectangles 12¹/₂" x 16¹/₂" for **pillow top backing** and **pillow backing**.

From light pink solid fabric:
- Cut 2 **medium flower petals**.
- Cut 1 **small flower petals**.

From pink solid fabric:
- Cut 2 **strips** 2¹/₂" x 13¹/₂".
- Cut 2 **strips** 2" x 12¹/₂".
- Cut 4 **medium flower petals**.
- Cut 2 **small flower petals**.

From dark pink solid fabric:
- Cut **bias strip** 3" x 68", pieced as needed for welting.
- Cut 2 **medium flower petals**.
- Cut 1 **small flower petal**.

From yellow solid fabric:
- Cut 3 **flower centers**.

From green solid fabric:
- Cut 6 **leaves** in any combination.

From brown solid fabric:
- Cut 3 **branches**.

Assembling the Pillow Top

Use a ¹/₄" seam allowance throughout. Use 3 strands of floss for all embroidery.

1. Fold 10" x 15" **rectangle** into quarters; press to mark placement guidelines and center.
2. Refer to **Pillow Top Diagram**, to pin appliqués in place.
3. Using brown floss for branches, pink floss for flowers, green floss for leaves, and yellow floss for centers, refer to **Hand Stitches**, page 96, to Blanket Stitch appliqués to background. Use brown floss to Stem Stitch detail lines in petals. Satin Stitch tips of petals, and Straight Stitch highlights in centers. Use green floss to Stem Stitch leaf stems and detail lines in leaves.

4. Trim appliquéd rectangle to 8½" x 13½".

5. Sew 2½" x 13½" strips to top and bottom of appliquéd rectangle. Sew remaining strips to sides of appliquéd rectangle.

6. Follow **Quilting**, page 87, to mark, layer, and quilt as desired. We outline quilted around all appliqués. We also stitched diagonal crosshatch quilting ⅞" apart across the background and borders.

7. Follow **Adding Welting To Pillow Top**, page 94, to make a welted pillow.

PILLOW TOP DIAGRAM

Dogwood
Wall Hanging

Finished Wall Hanging Size:
22" x 22" (56 cm x 56 cm)

Yardage Requirements

Yardage is based on 43"/44" (109 cm/112 cm) wide fabric with a usable width of 40" (102 cm).

- 1³/₄ yds (1.6 m) of cream solid fabric
- ¹/₈ yd (11 cm) of light pink solid fabric
- ³/₈ yd (34 cm) of pink solid fabric
- ¹/₈ yd (11 cm) of dark pink solid fabric
- ¹/₈ yd (11 cm) of yellow solid fabric
- ¹/₈ yd (11 cm) of green solid fabric
- ¹/₈ yd (11 cm) of brown solid fabric

You will also need:

- 26" x 26" (66 cm x 66 cm) piece of batting
- Embroidery floss - pink, yellow, green, and brown
- Water-soluble fabric marking pen

Cutting the Pieces

*Follow **Rotary Cutting**, page 80, to cut fabric. Cut all strips across the selvage-to-selvage width of the fabric unless otherwise indicated. All measurements include ¹/₄" seam allowances. Use patterns, pages 12 - 13, to cut appliqué pieces.*

From cream solid fabric:
- Cut 3 **binding strips** 2¹/₂"w.
- Cut 2 **strips** 1¹/₂" wide. Label each as A.
- Cut 2 **strips** 1¹/₂" wide. Label as D and E.
- Cut **backing** 26" x 26".
- Cut **top** 16" x 16".

From light pink solid fabric:
- Cut 2 **large flower petals**.
- Cut 4 **medium flower petals**.

From pink solid fabric:
- Cut 4 **strips** 1¹/₂" wide. Label two as B and two as C.
- Cut 1 **strip** 1¹/₂" wide. Label as F.
- Cut 4 **large flower petals**.
- Cut 8 **medium flower petals**.

From dark pink solid fabric:
- Cut 2 **large flower petals**.
- Cut 4 **medium flower petals**.

From yellow solid fabric:
- Cut 6 **flower centers**.

From green solid fabric:
- Cut 9 **leaves**.

From brown solid fabric:
- Cut 6 **branches**.

CELEBRATE THE SEASON OF RENEWAL WITH A RING OF
DOGWOOD BLOSSOMS! THIS FRESH-AS-SPRINGTIME WALL
HANGING HAS A WREATH OF THE PINK BLOOMS AT ITS
CENTER. IT'S SUCH A RESTFUL SIGHT; YOU MAY DECIDE
TO ENJOY THIS LITTLE QUILT ALL YEAR!

Assembling the Wall Hanging

*Follow **Machine Piecing**, page 81, and
Pressing, page 83. Use a $^1/_4$" seam allowance.
Use 3 strands of floss for all embroidery.*

1. Fold **top** into quarters; press to mark
   placement guidelines and center.
   Using fabric marking pen, mark an
   8" diameter circle in center of square.

2. Refer to **Wall Hanging Top Diagram**,
   to pin appliqués in place.

3. Using brown floss for branches, pink
   floss for flowers, green floss for leaves,
   and yellow floss for centers, refer to
   Hand Stitches, page 96, to Blanket
   Stitch appliqués to background. Use
   brown floss to Stem Stitch detail lines
   in petals. Satin Stitch tips of petals,
   and Straight Stitch highlights in
   centers. Use green floss to Stem Stitch
   detail lines in leaves.

4. Trim appliquéd top to $15^1/_2$" x $15^1/_2$".

5. Sew 1 each of **strips** A, B, and C
   together to make **Strip Set A**.
   Repeat with remaining A, B, and C
   strips to make 2 Strip Set A's. Cut
   across 1 Strip Set A at $1^1/_2$" intervals
   to make **Unit 1**. Make 4 Unit 1's. Cut
   across remainder of Strip Set A's at
   $15^1/_2$" intervals to make **Unit 2**. Make
   4 Unit 2's.

6. Sew 1 each of **strips** D, E, and F
   together to make **Strip Set B**. Cut
   across Strip Set B at $1^1/_2$" intervals to
   make **Unit 3**. Make 8 Unit 3's.

7. Sew 2 **Unit 3's** and 1 **Unit 1**
   together to make a **9-Patch Block**.
   Make 4 9-Patch Blocks.

8. Sew 1 Unit 2 to each side of
   appliquéd top. Sew 1 9-Patch
   Block to each side of remaining
   Unit 2's; sew to top and bottom of
   appliquéd top.

STRIP SET A
(MAKE 2)

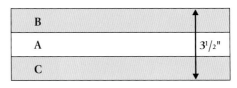

UNIT 1
(MAKE 4)

UNIT 2
(MAKE 4)

STRIP SET B

UNIT 3
(MAKE 8)

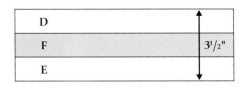

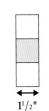

9-PATCH BLOCK
(MAKE 4)

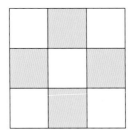

Completing the Wall Hanging

1. Follow **Quilting**, page 87, to mark, layer, and quilt as desired. We outline quilted around all appliqués. We also stitched diagonal crosshatch quilting $7/8$" apart in cream background. We also quilted in the ditch along all borders.

2. Follow **Making A Hanging Sleeve**, page 91, to attach hanging sleeve to wall hanging.

3. Follow **Making Straight-Grain Binding**, page 92, and use **binding strips** to make binding. Follow **Attaching Binding with Mitered Corners**, page 92, to attach binding to wall hanging.

WALL HANGING TOP DIAGRAM

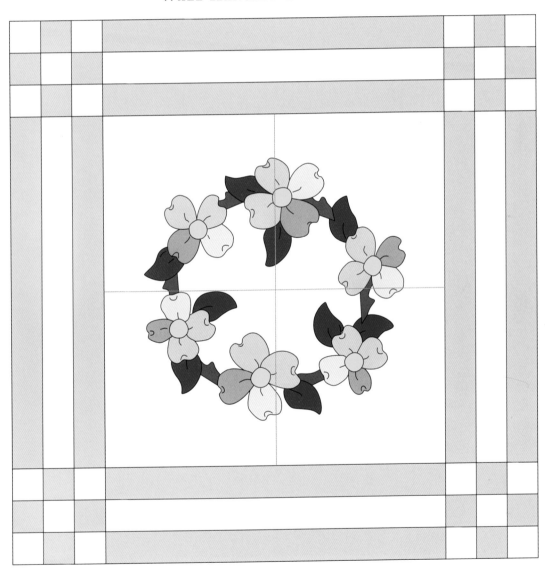

Palm Leaf
PILLOW

FINISHED PILLOW SIZE:
14" X 14" (36 CM X 36 CM)

Yardage Requirements

Yardage is based on 43"/44" (109 cm/112 cm) wide fabric with a usable width of 40" (102 cm).

    Assorted pink, blue, yellow, green, and
      purple print fabrics
    White solid fabric
    $1/2$ yd (46 cm) of fabric for backing

You will also need:

    14" x 14" (36 cm x 36 cm) pillow form
    Foundation paper (printer paper will do)

Cutting the Pieces

*Follow **Rotary Cutting**, page 80, to cut fabric. Cut all strips across the selvage-to-selvage width of the fabric unless otherwise indicated. All measurements include $1/4$" seam allowances.*

From *each* print fabric:

- Cut 1 strip $2^1/2$" wide. Randomly cut each strip in **lengths** varying from $1^1/2$" to 4".

THIS SPLASH OF SPRINGTIME COLOR IS JUST FOUR
EASY, FOUNDATION-PIECED BLOCKS AND A BORDER OF
SCRAP-HAPPY RECTANGLES. IN PASTELS, IT'S A JOYFUL
DESIGN FOR THE EASTER SEASON. CHOOSE GREEN AND
RED HUES TO CREATE A CHRISTMAS CACTUS PILLOW.

Assembling the Pillow Top

*Follow **Machine Piecing**, page 81, and **Pressing**, page 83. Use a ¹/₄" seam allowance unless otherwise stated.*

1. Photocopy patterns A and B and follow **Foundation Piecing**, page 82, to piece Units A and B. Foundation piece 4 of each Unit.

2. Sew 1 Unit A and 1 Unit B together to complete **Unit 1**. Make 4 Unit 1's.

3. Sew 4 Unit 1's together to complete Block.

UNIT A
(MAKE 4)

UNIT B
(MAKE 4)

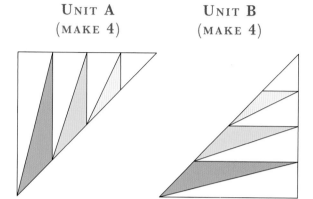

UNIT 1
(MAKE 4)

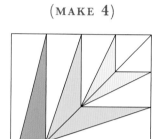

PILLOW TOP DIAGRAM

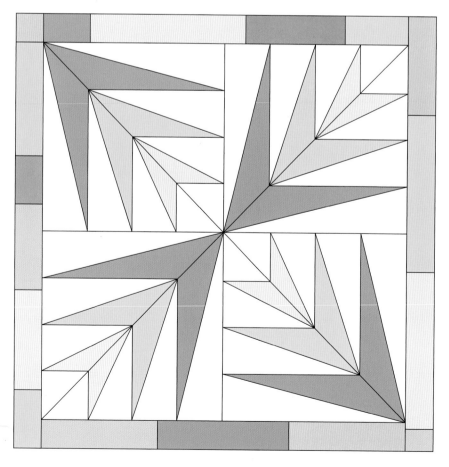

Completing the Pillow Top

1. For pieced borders, piece **lengths** together to form 2 **short borders** 2½" x 10½" and two **long borders** 2½" x 14½".

2. Sew short borders to opposite sides of Block. Sew long borders to remaining sides of Block.

2. Follow **Making a Knife-Edge Pillow**, page 95, to complete pillow.

PATTERNS

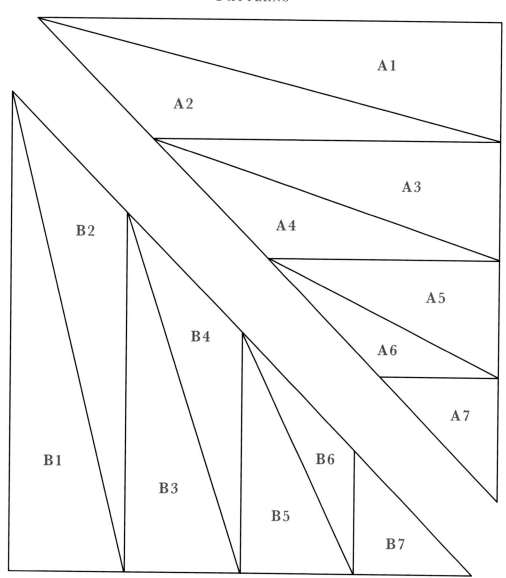

Leisure Arts grants permission to the owner of this book to photocopy the patterns on this page for personal use only.

Grandmother's
FLOWER GARDEN PILLOW

FINISHED PILLOW SIZE:
12" x 12" (30 CM X 30 CM)

Yardage Requirements

Yardage is based on 43"/44" (109 cm/112 cm) wide fabric with a usable width of 40" (102 cm).

Scraps of pink, blue, and yellow print fabrics

$1^3/_8$ yds (1.3 m) of white solid fabric for background, backing, and ruffle

$^1/_2$ yd (46 cm) of fabric for welting

You will also need:

12" x 12" (30 cm x 30 cm) pillow form

$1^3/_4$ yds (1.6 m) of $^1/_4$" (6 mm) diameter cord

Freezer paper

Cutting the Pieces

Follow Rotary Cutting, page 80, to cut fabric. Cut all strips across the selvage-to-selvage width of the fabric unless otherwise indicated. All measurements include $^1/_4$" seam allowances.

From freezer paper:
- Use dashed line on pattern, page 28, to cut 19 **hexagons**.

From *each* print fabric:
- Use solid line on pattern to cut:
  - 1 yellow **hexagon**.
  - 6 pink **hexagons**.
  - 12 blue **hexagons**.

From white solid fabric:
- Cut 2 squares $12^1/_2$" x $12^1/_2$" for **background** and **pillow back**.
- Cut 7" x 120" **bias strip** for ruffle, pieced as needed.

THIS FRESH PILLOW IS A GREAT OPPORTUNITY TO TRY
YOUR HAND AT ENGLISH PAPER PIECING. HAND STITCHING
AROUND A FREEZER-PAPER TEMPLATE ENSURES STRAIGHT,
ACCURATE SEAMS. AND SINCE THERE ARE ONLY NINETEEN
HEXAGONS TO SEW AND THE FINISHED FLOWER SHAPE IS
APPLIQUÉD TO A WHITE BACKGROUND (NO BACKGROUND
PIECING!), THE PILLOW TOP GOES TOGETHER QUICKLY.
THE WELTING AND RUFFLE EDGING ARE A CLASSIC FINISH.

Assembling the Pillow Top

*Follow **Pressing**, page 83. Use a $1/4$" seam allowance.*

1. Place 1 freezer paper **hexagon** on the wrong side of one fabric **hexagon**, with the waxy side of the freezer paper facing up. Use a warm, dry iron to press the seam allowances onto the paper. Repeat for remaining hexagons.

2. Matching right sides and all corners, place yellow and 1 pink hexagon together as shown in **Fig. 1**. Avoiding stitching through the paper, whipstitch two edges together from corner to corner along one side, backstitching at the beginning and end of the seam. Open pieces flat **(Fig. 2)**.

HEXAGON

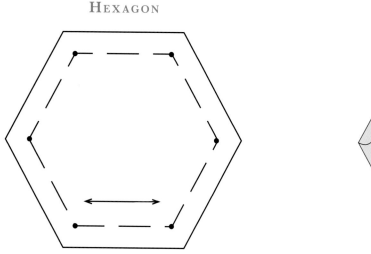

FIG. 1

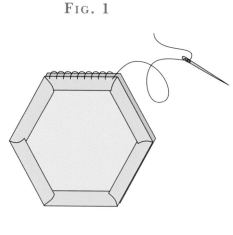

FIG. 2

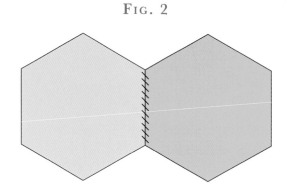

3. Continue adding pink hexagons to the yellow hexagon, one at a time, in the same manner to make **Unit 1**. It is not necessary to knot and clip your thread each time you reach the end of a hexagon side.

4. Sew a second ring of blue hexagons around Unit 1 to make **Unit 2**.

5. Remove the freezer paper from the hexagons. Follow **Hand Stitches**, page 96, to center and Blind Stitch Unit 2 to **background** to make **Pillow Top**.

UNIT 1

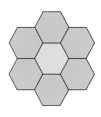

UNIT 2

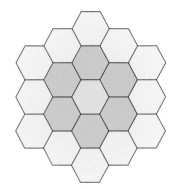

PILLOW TOP

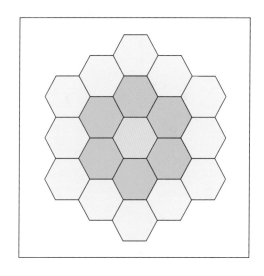

Completing the Pillow Top

1. Join ends of **bias strip** for ruffle to make a continuous loop.

2. Follow **Pillow Finishing**, page 94, to make a ruffled pillow with welting.

Pot of Lilies
PILLOW

FINISHED PILLOW SIZE:
12" x 12" (30 CM x 30 CM)

Yardage Requirements

Yardage is based on 43"/44" (109 cm/112 cm) wide fabric with a usable width of 40" (102 cm).

Assorted pink, blue, yellow, green, and
purple print and solid fabrics
White solid fabric
$^3/_8$ yd (34 cm) of fabric for backing
$^1/_2$ yd (46 cm) of fabric for welting

You will also need:

12" x 12" (30 cm x 30 cm) pillow form
$1^3/_4$ yds (1.6 m) of $^1/_4$" (6 mm)
diameter cord

Cutting the Pieces

*Follow **Rotary Cutting**, page 80, to cut fabric. Cut all strips across the selvage-to-selvage width of the fabric unless otherwise indicated. All measurements include $^1/_4$" seam allowances.*

From purple print fabric:

- Cut 2 **side borders** $1^1/_2$" x $10^1/_2$".
- Cut 2 **top** and **bottom borders** $1^1/_2$" x $12^1/_2$".

From white solid fabric:

- Cut 2 squares $5^7/_8$" x $5^7/_8$". Cut each square diagonally to make 4 **background triangles**.

SURPRISE—IT'S EASY! WE THINK
YOU'LL LOVE HOW SIMPLE IT IS TO
SEW THIS POT OF LILIES PILLOW.
THE DESIGN IS FOUNDATION-PIECED
ON PAPER, SO THERE'S NO TEDIOUS
CUTTING OF ALL THE DIFFERENT
SHAPES. ADD A MATCHING-COLOR
BORDER (OR MIX IT UP FOR
CONTRAST), AND YOUR PILLOW
WILL BLOOM FOR YEARS.

Assembling the Pillow Top

*Follow **Machine Piecing**, page 81, and **Pressing**, page 83. Use a ¹/₄" seam allowance.*

1. Photocopy patterns A-F and follow **Foundation Piecing**, page 82, to piece **Units A-F**.
2. Sew Units together to complete **Unit 1**.
3. Sew 1 **background triangle** to each side of Unit 1 to make **Unit 2**.

Completing the Pillow Top

1. Sew **side**, then **top** and **bottom borders** to Unit 2 to complete **Pillow Top**.
2. Follow **Adding Welting To Pillow Top**, page 94, to make a welted pillow.

UNIT 1

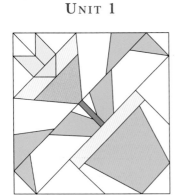

UNIT 2

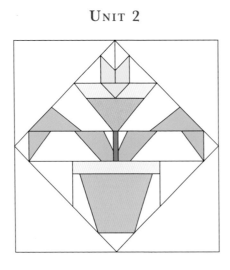

PILLOW TOP

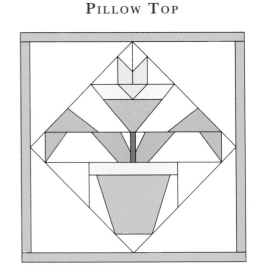

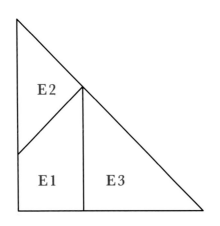

E 2

E 1   E 3

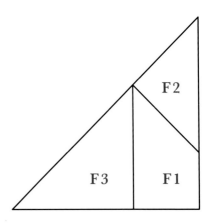

F 2

F 3   F 1

Leisure Arts grants permission to the owner of this book to photocopy the patterns on this page for personal use only.

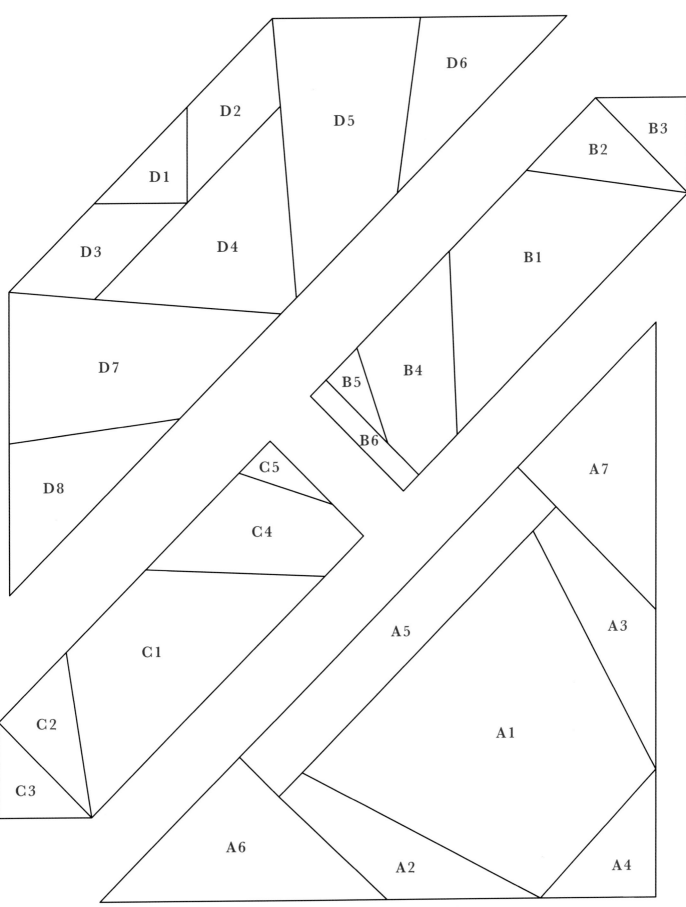

D6

D2

D5

D1

B2

B3

D3

D4

B1

D7

B5

B4

B6

C5

A7

D8

C4

A3

A5

C1

A1

C2

C3

A6

A2

A4

Leisure Arts grants permission to the owner of this book to photocopy the patterns on this page for personal use only.

Sampler
WALL HANGING

FINISHED WALL HANGING SIZE:
15" x 15" (38 CM x 38 CM)

Yardage Requirements

Yardage is based on 43"/44" (109 cm/112 cm) wide fabric with a usable width of 40" (102 cm).

$^1/_4$ yd (23 cm) of light tan print fabric
$^1/_4$ yd (23 cm) of rust print fabric
$^1/_4$ yd (23 cm) of dark rust print fabric
$^1/_4$ yd (23 cm) of dark gold plaid fabric
$^1/_4$ yd (23 cm) of tan print fabric
Scraps of assorted prints for flower and
   flowerpot appliqués
$^5/_8$ yd (57 cm) of fabric for backing and
   hanging sleeve
$^1/_4$ yd (23 cm) of fabric for binding

You will also need:

19" x 19" (48 cm x 48 cm) piece of batting
Heavy-duty paper-backed fusible web

THIS WEE WALL HANGING OR TABLE TOPPER IS A TINY
TREAT! A TRADITIONAL BASKET BLOCK PARTNERS WITH
THREE OF APPLIQUÉ TO MAKE A GARDEN-THEMED SPLASH
OF COLOR. IT'S PERFECT FOR ANY DÉCOR!

Cutting the Pieces

*Follow **Rotary Cutting**, page 80, to cut fabric. Cut all strips across the selvage-to-selvage width of the fabric unless otherwise indicated. All measurements include $^1/_4$" seam allowances.*

From light tan print fabric:
- Cut 1 A $4^1/_2$" x $3^3/_4$".
- Cut 1 C $3^3/_4$" x $3^3/_4$".
- Cut 1 G $3^3/_4$" x $4^1/_4$".
- Cut 1 square $4^5/_8$" x $4^5/_8$". Cut square once diagonally to make 2 **large triangles** (you will need 1 and have 1 left over).
- Cut 1 square $2^3/_8$" x $2^3/_8$". Cut square once diagonally to make 2 **medium triangles** (you will need 1 and have 1 left over).
- Cut 2 **rectangles** $1^1/_4$" x $3^1/_2$".

From rust print fabric:
- Cut 1 strip $1^1/_2$"w. From this strip, cut 2 **top/bottom inner borders** $1^1/_2$" x 9" and 2 **side inner borders** $1^1/_2$" x 11".
- Cut 1 B $1^1/_4$" x $4^1/_2$".
- Cut 1 E $1^3/_4$" x $4^1/_2$".
- Cut 1 F $1^1/_4$" x $3^3/_4$".
- Cut 1 H $1^1/_4$" x 5".

From dark rust print fabric:
- Cut 2 strips $2^1/_2$"w. From these strips, cut 2 **side outer borders** $2^1/_2$" x 15" and 2 **top/bottom outer borders** $2^1/_2$" x 11".

From dark gold plaid fabric:
- Cut 5 **large squares** $1^3/_4$" x $1^3/_4$".
- Cut 4 squares $1^5/_8$" x $1^5/_8$". Cut squares once diagonally to make 8 **small triangles** (you will need 7 and have 1 left over).

From tan print fabric:
- Cut 5 **large squares** $1^3/_4$" x $1^3/_4$".
- Cut 1 **small square** $1^1/_4$" x $1^1/_4$".

From scraps of assorted prints:
- Cut 1 D $1^1/_4$" x $3^3/_4$".
- Use patterns, page 39, and follow Steps 1-3 of **Preparing Fusible Appliqués**, page 84, to cut 1 **A** appliqué for basket handle and remaining desired **appliqués**. (For the flowers in the pot we made appliqués by fusing web to the wrong side of a floral print fabric and cutting the flower shapes from the fabric.)

From fabric for binding:
- Cut 2 **binding strips** 2"w.

Assembling the Wall Hanging Top

*Follow **Machine Piecing**, page 81, and **Pressing**, page 83. Use a ¹/₄" seam allowance.*

1. Draw a diagonal line on wrong side of each tan **large square**. With right sides together, place 1 marked tan large square on top of 1 dark gold **large square**. Stitch ¹/₄" from each side of drawn line (**Fig. 1**).

2. Cut along drawn line and press seam allowances toward darker fabric to make 2 **triangle-squares**. Trim each triangle-square to 1¹/₄" x 1¹/₄". Make 10 triangle-squares. You will use 9 and have 1 left over.

3. Sew 9 triangle-squares, 5 dark gold **small triangles**, and 1 tan **small square** together to make Rows **A**, **B**, **C**, **D**, and **E**. Sew **Rows** together to make **Unit 1**.

4. Referring to **Unit 2**, fuse **basket handle** to **large triangle**, making sure end of handle extends into seam allowance.

5. Sew 1 **Unit 1** and large triangle with handle together to make **Unit 2**.

6. Sew 1 **rectangle** and 1 **small triangle** together to make **Unit 3**. Sew 1 **small triangle** and 1 **rectangle** together to make **Unit 4**.

7. Sew 1 **Unit 2**, 1 **Unit 3**, 1 **Unit 4**, and 1 **medium triangle** together to make **Basket Block**.

8. Sew **A** and **B** together to make **Unit 5**. Sew **C**, **D**, and **E** together to make **Unit 6**. Sew **F**, **G**, and **H** together to make **Unit 7**.

9. Sew **Unit 5**, **Unit 6**, **Unit 7**, and **Basket Block** together to make center section of wall hanging top.

10. Follow manufacturer's instructions to fuse **appliqués** to center section.

11. Sew **top**, **bottom**, then **side inner borders** to center section. Repeat with **outer borders** to complete **Wall Hanging Top**.

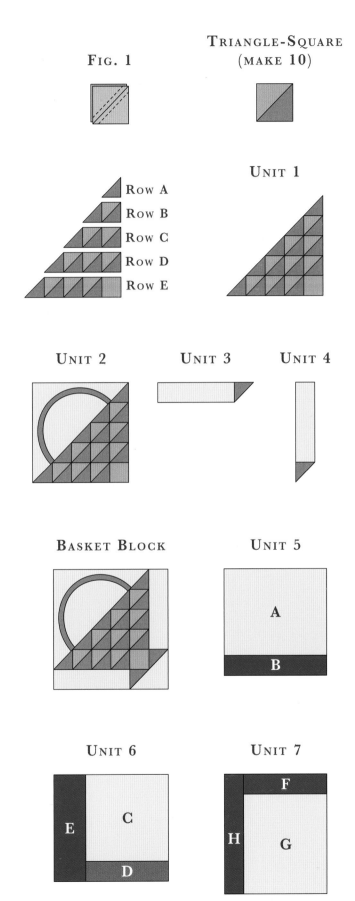

FIG. 1

TRIANGLE-SQUARE
(MAKE 10)

ROW A
ROW B
ROW C
ROW D
ROW E

UNIT 1

UNIT 2   UNIT 3   UNIT 4

BASKET BLOCK   UNIT 5

A
B

UNIT 6   UNIT 7

E   C   D   F   H   G

Completing the Wall Hanging

1. Follow **Quilting**, page 87, to mark, layer, and quilt. Our wall hanging is hand quilted in the ditch along the inner border and along each section divider.
2. Follow **Making A Hanging Sleeve**, page 91, to attach hanging sleeve to wall hanging.
3. Follow **Making Straight-Grain Binding**, page 92, and use **binding strips** to make binding. Follow **Attaching Binding with Mitered Corners**, page 92, to attach binding to quilt.

WALL HANGING TOP

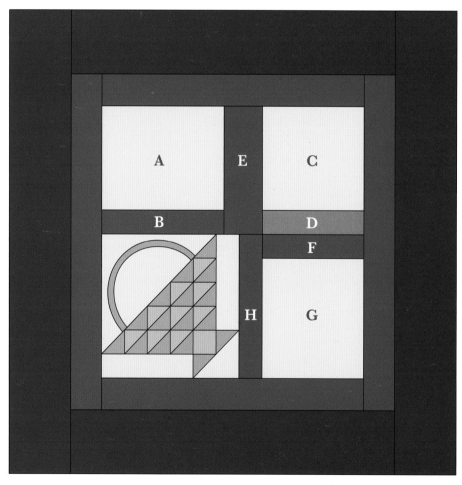

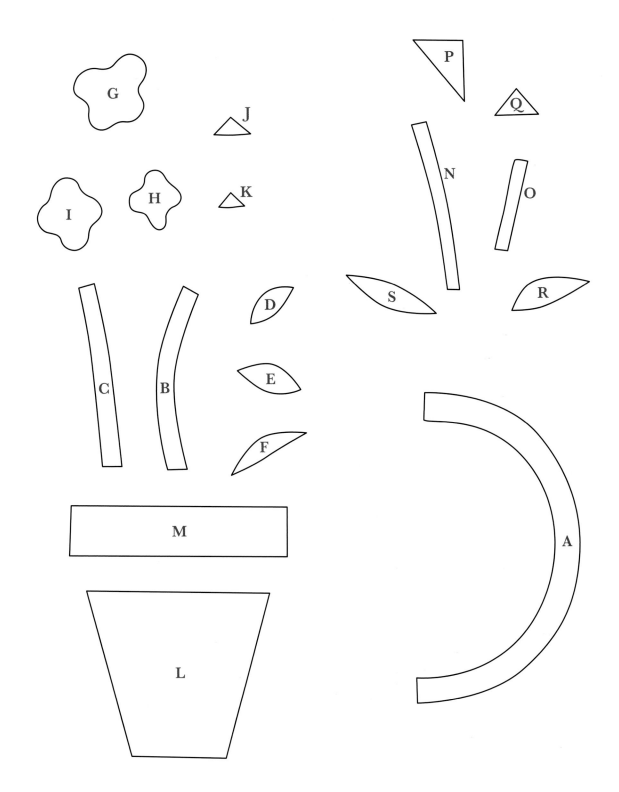

Pastel Posies
QUILT

FINISHED QUILT SIZE:
88$\frac{1}{2}$" x 96$\frac{1}{2}$" (225 CM X 245 CM)

FINISHED BLOCK SIZE:
8" x 8" (20 CM X 20 CM)

Yardage Requirements

Yardage is based on 43"/44" (109 cm/112 cm) wide fabric with a usable width of 40" (102 cm).

- 6 yds (5.5 m) of white print fabric
- 4$\frac{1}{4}$ yds (3.9 m) of floral print fabric
- $\frac{7}{8}$ yd (80 cm) of green solid fabric
- 2$\frac{5}{8}$ yds (2.4 m) of pink print fabric
- $\frac{5}{8}$ yd (57 cm) of light pink solid fabric
- 8 yds (7.3 m) of fabric for backing
- 1 yd (91 cm) of fabric for binding

You will also need:

- 96$\frac{1}{2}$" x 104$\frac{1}{2}$" (245 cm x 265 cm) piece of batting
- Paper-backed fusible web
- Transparent monofilament thread for appliqué

Cutting the Pieces

*Follow **Rotary Cutting**, page 80, to cut fabric. Cut all strips across the selvage-to-selvage width of the fabric unless otherwise indicated. Borders are cut longer than necessary and will be trimmed to fit quilt top center. All measurements include $\frac{1}{4}$" seam allowances.*

From white print fabric:
- Cut 20 **wide strips** 3$\frac{1}{2}$"w.
- Cut 14 strips 9"w. From these strips, cut 55 **large squares** 9" x 9".

From floral print fabric:
- Cut 10 **narrow strips** 2$\frac{1}{2}$"w.
- Cut 8 **wide strips** 3$\frac{1}{2}$"w.
- Cut 2 *lengthwise* **side outer borders** 3$\frac{1}{2}$" x 94".
- Cut 2 *lengthwise* **top/bottom outer borders** 3$\frac{1}{2}$" x 92".

From green solid fabric:
- Cut 2 **side inner borders** 1$\frac{1}{4}$" x 92$\frac{1}{2}$", pieced as needed.
- Cut 2 **top/bottom inner borders** 1$\frac{1}{4}$" x 86", pieced as needed.

From pink print fabric:
- Cut 20 strips 3$\frac{1}{2}$"w. From these strips, cut 220 **medium squares** 3$\frac{1}{2}$" x 3$\frac{1}{2}$".
- Cut 4 **narrow strips** 2$\frac{1}{2}$"w.

FOR THIS CHEERFUL QUILT, CHOOSE THE BORDER FABRIC
FIRST! ANY MEDIUM- TO LARGE-SCALE FLORAL PRINT WILL
WORK, AND ONCE YOU KNOW WHICH PRINT YOU'LL USE,
IT'S A SIMPLE MATTER TO PICK THE REST OF THE FABRICS.
THIS DESIGN IS ESPECIALLY SWEET FOR A GIRL'S ROOM.

FIG. 1

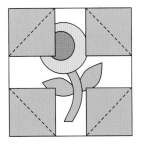

FIG. 2

FIG. 3

BLOCK A
(MAKE 55)

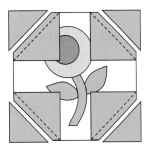

Preparing the Appliqués

Use patterns, page 44, and follow
Preparing Fusible Appliqués,
page 84, to cut appliqués.

From light pink solid fabric:
- Cut 55 **large circles**.

From pink print fabric:
- Cut 55 **small circles**.

From green solid fabric:
- Cut 55 **leaves**.
- Cut 55 **stems**.

Assembling the Quilt Top

Follow **Machine Piecing**, *page 81, and*
Pressing, *page 83. Use a* $^1/_4$" *seam
allowance.*

1. Referring to **Fig. 1**, arrange appliqué pieces on **large squares**; fuse in place.

2. Follow **Satin Stitch Appliqué**, page 84, to use technique to stitch appliqués to center of large squares using monofilament thread, a narrow stitch width, and a short stitch length. Trim each large square to $8^1/_2$" x $8^1/_2$".

3. Place 1 **medium square** on each corner of 1 large square with right sides together and stitch diagonally as shown in **Fig. 2**. Trim $^1/_4$" from stitching lines as shown in **Fig. 3**. Press open, pressing seam allowances toward darker fabric to make **Block A**. Make 55 Block A's.

4. Sew 2 white print **wide strips** and 1 floral print **narrow strip** together to make **Strip Set A**. Make 10 Strip Set A's. Cut across Strip Set A's at 3¹/₂" intervals to make 110 **Unit 1's**.

5. Sew 2 floral print **wide strips** and 1 pink print **narrow strip** together to make **Strip Set B**. Make 4 Strip Set B's. Cut across Strip Set B's at 2¹/₂" intervals to make 55 **Unit 2's**.

6. Sew 2 **Unit 1's** and 1 **Unit 2** together to make **Block B**. Make 55 Block B's.

7. Sew 5 **Block A's** and 5 **Block B's** together to make **Row A**. Make 6 Row A's.

8. Sew 5 **Block B's** and 5 **Block A's** together to make **Row B**. Make 5 Row B's.

9. Referring to **Quilt Top Diagram**, page 45, sew Row A's and Row B's together to make center section of quilt top.

10. Follow **Adding Squared Borders**, page 86, to sew **side**, then **top** and **bottom inner borders** to center section. Add **side**, then **top** and **bottom outer borders** to complete **Quilt Top**.

STRIP SET A
(MAKE 10)

UNIT 1
(MAKE 110)

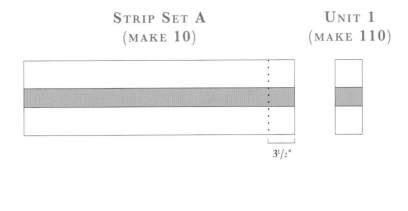

3¹/₂"

STRIP SET B
(MAKE 4)

UNIT 2
(MAKE 55)

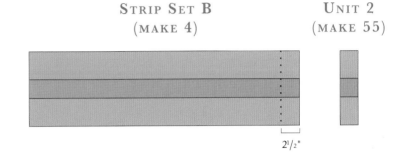

2¹/₂"

BLOCK B
(MAKE 55)

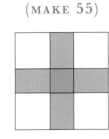

ROW A
(MAKE 6)

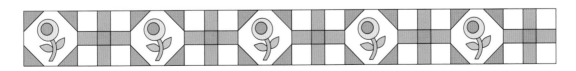

ROW B
(MAKE 5)

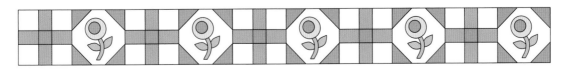

Completing the Quilt

1. Follow **Quilting**, page 87, to mark, layer, and quilt. Our quilt is hand quilted with outline quilting along the seams and around the appliqués in the Block A's and an X across the Block B's. The borders are crosshatch quilted.

2. Cut a 33" square of binding fabric. Follow **Making Continuous Bias Strip Binding**, page 91, to make $2^1/_2$"w bias binding. Follow **Attaching Binding with Mitered Corners**, page 92, to attach binding to quilt.

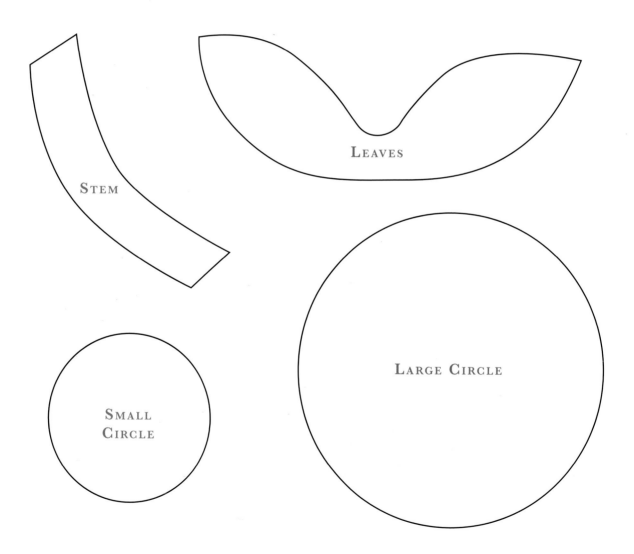

STEM

LEAVES

SMALL CIRCLE

LARGE CIRCLE

Springtime
BABY QUILT

FINISHED QUILT SIZE:
40$\frac{1}{2}$" x 50$\frac{1}{2}$" (103 CM x 128 CM)

Yardage Requirements

Yardage is based on 43"/44" (109 cm/112 cm) wide fabric with a usable width of 40" (102 cm).

- 1$\frac{5}{8}$ yds (1.5 m) of white print fabric
- $\frac{3}{8}$ yd (34 cm) of yellow check fabric
- $\frac{1}{4}$ yd (23 cm) of green stripe fabric
- $\frac{1}{4}$ yd (23 m) *each* of purple check, stripe, and dot fabrics
- 3$\frac{1}{4}$ yds (3 m) of fabric for backing
- $\frac{3}{4}$ yd (69 cm) of fabric for binding

You will also need:

- 48$\frac{1}{2}$" x 58$\frac{1}{2}$" (123 cm x 149 cm) piece of batting
- Paper-backed fusible web
- Transparent monofilament thread for appliqué
- Template plastic
- Craft knife
- Green fabric paint
- Stencil brush

BABY LOVES SPRINGTIME, TOO! THIS WARM AND COLORFUL
BLANKET IS SPRINKLED WITH HEARTS SO THAT SPECIAL
CHILD WILL ALWAYS KNOW HOW MUCH YOU CARE. MACHINE
APPLIQUÉ AND ROTARY CUTTING WILL SPEED YOU ON YOUR
WAY TO COMPLETING THIS ADORABLE QUILT.

Cutting the Pieces

*Follow **Rotary Cutting**, page 80, to cut fabric. Cut all strips across the selvage-to-selvage width of the fabric unless otherwise indicated. All measurements include ¹/₄" seam allowances.*

From white print fabric:
- Cut 2 **strips** 2¹/₂"w.
- Cut 2 **side outer borders** 6¹/₂" x 36¹/₂".
- Cut 2 **top/bottom outer borders** 6¹/₂" x 26¹/₂".
- Cut 2 **panels** 9¹/₂" x 26¹/₂".

From yellow check fabric:
- Cut 4 **strips** 2¹/₂"w.

From green stripe fabric:
- Cut 1 strip 1¹/₄"w. From this strip, cut 4 **border pieces** 1¹/₄" x 6¹/₂".
- Cut 2 **top/bottom inner borders** 1¹/₄" x 40".
- Cut 2 **side inner borders** 1¹/₄" x 36¹/₂".

From purple check, stripe, and dot print fabric:
- Cut 2 **strips** 2¹/₂"w from **each** fabric.

From fabric for binding:
- Cut 2 **top/bottom binding strips** 4" x 40" and 2 **side binding strips** 4" x 53", pieced as necessary.

Assembling the Quilt Top

*Follow **Machine Piecing**, page 81, and **Pressing**, page 83. Use a ¹/₄" seam allowance.*

1. (**Note:** *Measurements for stencil placement on **Quilt Top Diagram**, page 50, do not include seam allowances.*) Referring to **Quilt Top Diagram**, use **Stem Stencil** pattern, page 51, and follow **Stenciling**, page 95, to stencil stems on **outer borders**. Stencil stems on **panels**, using only 2 segments of stem stencil for each design area.

2. Use patterns and follow **Preparing Fusible Appliqués**, page 84, to cut 10 **Hearts** and 2 **Flower Petals** from purple check, 4 **Flower Petals** from purple stripe, 2 **Flower Petals** from purple dot, 4 **Flower Petals** from yellow check, and 32 **Leaves** and 4 **Flower Bases** from green stripe. Follow **Satin Stitch Appliqué**, page 84, to use technique to stitch appliqués to panels and outer borders.

3. Sew purple dot and yellow check **strips** together to make **Strip Set A**. Make 2 Strip Set A's. Cut across Strip Set A's at 2¹/₂" intervals to make 29 **Unit 1's**. Repeat with purple check, white print, and purple stripe to make 2 **Strip Set B's** and 22 **Unit 2's**.

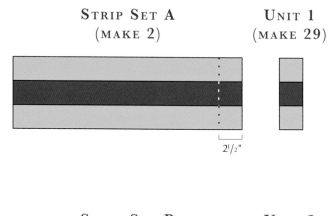

STRIP SET A
(MAKE 2)

2¹/₂"

UNIT 1
(MAKE 29)

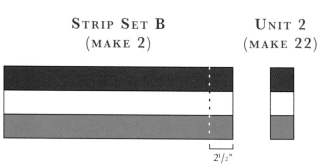

STRIP SET B
(MAKE 2)

2¹/₂"

UNIT 2
(MAKE 22)

4. Sew 7 **Unit 1's** and 6 **Unit 2's** together to make **Row**. Make 3 Rows.

5. Sew 2 **Unit 1's** and 1 **Unit 2** together to make **Border Square**. Make 4 Border Squares.

6. Referring to **Quilt Top Diagram**, sew **Rows** and **panels** together to make center section of quilt top.

7. Sew **side inner borders**, then **side outer borders** to center section.

8. Sew 2 **Border Squares**, 2 **border pieces**, and 1 **top/bottom outer border** together to make **Border Unit**. Make 2 Border Units.

9. Sew **top/bottom inner borders**, then **Border Units** to center section to complete **Quilt Top**.

ROW
(MAKE 3)

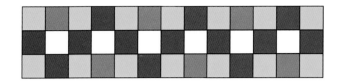

BORDER SQUARE
(MAKE 4)

QUILTING DIAGRAM

Completing the Quilt

1. Follow **Quilting**, page 87, to mark, layer, and quilt using **Quilting Diagram**, page 49, as a suggestion. Our quilt is hand quilted.

2. Matching wrong sides and raw edges, press each binding strip in half lengthwise. Follow **Attaching Binding with Overlapped Corners**, page 93, to attach binding to quilt.

QUILT TOP DIAGRAM

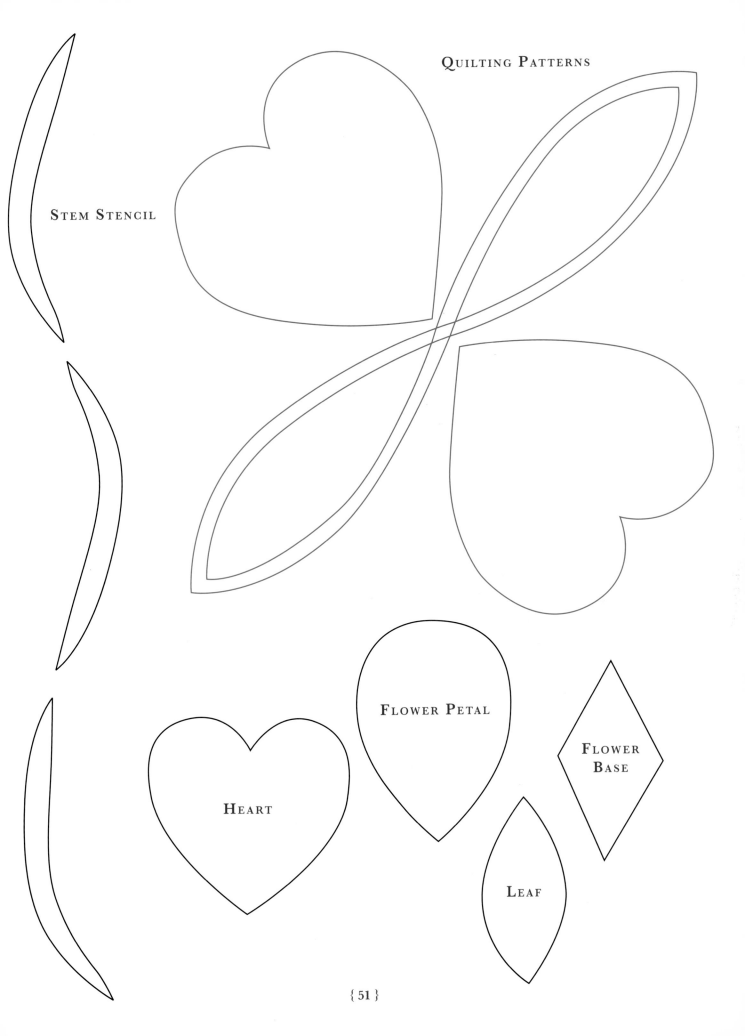

Stem Stencil

Flower Petal

Flower Base

Heart

Leaf

Pansy
WALL HANGING

FINISHED WALL HANGING SIZE:
$30^1/2$" x 44" (77 CM X 112 CM)

FINISHED BLOCK SIZE:
11" x 11" (28 CM X 28 CM)

Yardage Requirements

*Yardage is based on 43"/44" (109 cm/112 cm)
wide fabric with a usable width of 40" (102 cm).
A fat quarter measures approximately
18" x 22" (46 cm x 56 cm).*

$1^1/2$ yds (1.4 m) of purple solid fabric
$^3/_4$ yd (69 cm) of white solid fabric
$^1/_2$ yd (46 cm) of dark green solid fabric
1 fat quarter **each** of light green, very light
  purple, light purple, purple, dark purple,
  navy, light yellow, yellow, and dark yellow
$1^1/2$ yds (1.4 m) of fabric for backing and
  hanging sleeve
$^5/_8$ yd (57 cm) of fabric for binding

You will also need:

35" x 48" (89 cm x 122 cm) piece of batting
Template plastic
$^1/_4$" (6 mm) wide bias pressing bar
Purple embroidery floss

Cutting the Pieces

*Follow **Rotary Cutting**, page 80, to cut fabric. Cut
all strips across the selvage-to-selvage width of the
fabric unless otherwise indicated. Borders are cut
longer than necessary and will be trimmed to fit
quilt top center. All measurements include
$^1/_4$" seam allowances.*

From purple solid fabric:

- Cut 2 *lengthwise* **side borders** 3" x $47^1/2$".
- Cut 1 *lengthwise* **long sashing strip**
  3" x $38^1/2$".
- Cut 2 *lengthwise* **top/bottom borders**
  3" x 34".
- Cut 4 **short sashing strips** 3" x $11^1/2$".

From white solid fabric:

- Cut 2 strips $11^1/2$"w.
  From these strips, cut
  6 background squares
  $11^1/2$" x $11^1/2$".

From dark green solid fabric:

- Cut 1 **square**
  $16^1/2$" x $16^1/2$" for
  bias strip.

COLORFUL APPLIQUÉS INVITE
EVERYONE TO ENJOY THEIR
BEAUTY. EACH BLOCK IS
ECHO-QUILTED, MAKING THE
BOUQUETS APPEAR TO DANCE
IN A SPRING BREEZE.

[53]

Assembling the Wall Hanging Top

*Follow **Machine Piecing**, page 81, and **Pressing**, page 83. Use a $1/4$" seam allowance.*

1. Use patterns, page 57, and follow Step 1 of **Template Cutting**, page 81, to make 1 template for *each* of patterns **A-L**.

2. Using **Block Diagram**, page 55, as a suggestion for fabric colors, refer to **Needle-Turn Appliqué**, page 83, to make appliqués. For each Block, you will need:

4 A's	3 G's
4 B's	2 H's
4 C's	2 I's
3 D's (1 in reverse)	1 J
3 E's (1 in reverse)	2 K's (1 in reverse)
3 F's (1 in reverse)	2 L's (1 in reverse)

3. To make bias tube for stems, use **square** and follow Steps 1-6 of **Making Continuous Bias Strip Binding**, page 91, to make 1"w continuous bias strip.

4. Fold bias strip in half lengthwise with wrong sides together; do not press. Stitch $1/4$" from long raw edges to form tube; trim seam allowances to $1/8$". Place bias pressing bar inside 1 end of tube. Center seam at back of bar and press as you move bar down length of tube. Cut tube to desired lengths for stems.

5. Following **Block** diagram to layer and arrange appliqués and stem pieces on **background square**, refer to **Needle-Turn Appliqué** to stitch appliqués to background square to complete **Block**. Make 6 Blocks.

6. On each **Block**, use 3 strands of embroidery floss and **Satin Stitch**, page 96, to work a $1/4$" circle in the center of each open pansy.

7. Sew 3 **Blocks** and 2 **short sashing strips** together to make vertical **Row**. Make 2 Rows.

8. Sew **Rows** and **long sashing strip** together to make center section of wall hanging.

9. Referring to **Wall Hanging Top Diagram**, page 55, follow **Adding Mitered Borders**, page 86, to add **borders** to complete **Wall Hanging Top**.

BLOCK
(MAKE 6)

ROW
(MAKE 2)

WALL HANGING TOP DIAGRAM

Completing the Wall Hanging

1. Follow **Quilting**, page 87, to mark, layer, and quilt wall hanging using **Quilting Diagram** as a suggestion. Our wall hanging is hand quilted.

2. Follow **Making A Hanging Sleeve**, page 91, to attach hanging sleeve to wall hanging.

3. Cut an 18" square of binding fabric. Follow **Making Continuous Bias Strip Binding**, page 91, to make 1^1/$_2$"w bias binding. Follow **Attaching Binding with Mitered Corners**, page 92, to attach binding to quilt.

QUILTING DIAGRAM

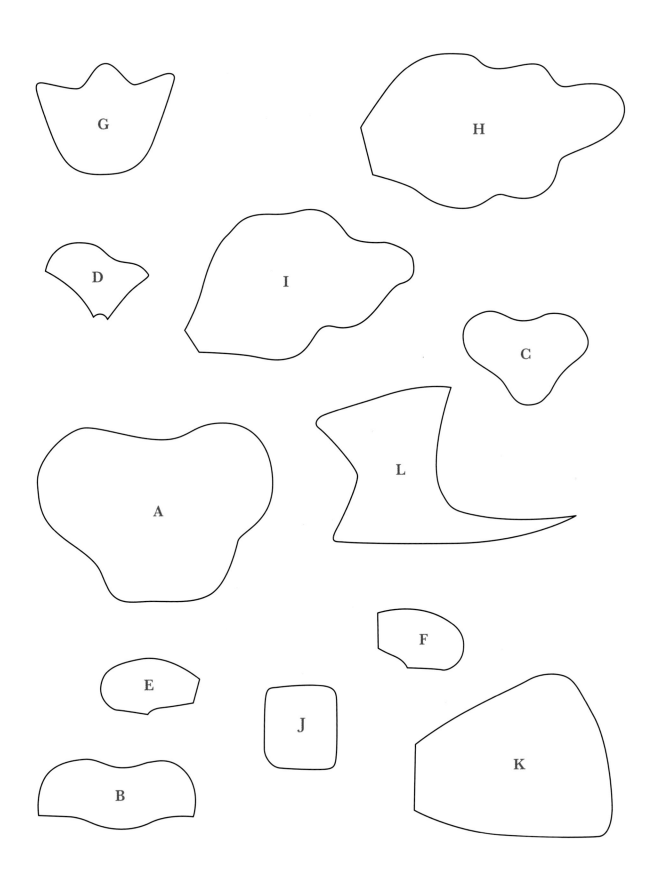

Vase of Flowers
B A B Y   Q U I L T

FINISHED QUILT SIZE:
45" x 50" (114 CM X 127 CM)

Yardage Requirements

Yardage is based on 43"/44" (109 cm/112 cm) wide fabric with a usable width of 40" (102 cm).

2³/₄ yds (2.5 m) of white solid fabric
¹/₂ yd (46 cm) of light blue print fabric
¹/₂ yd (46 cm) of blue print fabric
¹/₄ yd (23 cm) of light blue check fabric
¹/₈ yd (11 cm) of dark blue print fabric
3¹/₄ yds (3 m) of fabric for backing
⁵/₈ yd (57 cm) of fabric for binding

You will also need:

53" x 58" (135 cm x 147 cm) piece
  of batting
Paper-backed fusible web
Transparent monofilament thread
Water-soluble fabric marking pen

Cutting the Pieces

*Follow **Rotary Cutting**, page 80, to cut fabric. Cut all strips across the selvage-to-selvage width of the fabric unless otherwise indicated. All measurements include ¹/₄" seam allowances.*

From white solid fabric:
- Cut 1 **rectangle** 18¹/₂" x 23¹/₂" for medallion background.
- Cut 2 **side outer borders** 6¹/₂" x 37¹/₂".
- Cut 2 **top/bottom outer borders** 6¹/₂" x 32¹/₂".
- Cut 2 **side appliqué panels** 7¹/₂" x 26¹/₂".
- Cut 2 **top/bottom appliqué panels** 7¹/₂" x 21¹/₂".
- Cut 2 strips 6¹/₂"w. From these strips, cut 8 **corner squares** 6¹/₂" x 6¹/₂".

From light blue print fabric:
- Cut 2 **side inner borders** 2" x 25¹/₂".
- Cut 2 **top/bottom inner borders** 2" x 17¹/₂".

CREATE THIS LITTLE BABY QUILT
AND YOU'LL NOT ONLY MAKE A VERY
WELCOME GIFT, YOU'LL BE FASHIONING
A KEEPSAKE. FROM THE BEAUTIFUL
APPLIQUÉ TO THE SCALLOPED BORDER,
THIS HEIRLOOM-QUALITY DESIGN WILL
CAPTURE ALL THE LOVE YOU FEEL FOR
THE NEWEST MEMBER OF THE FAMILY.

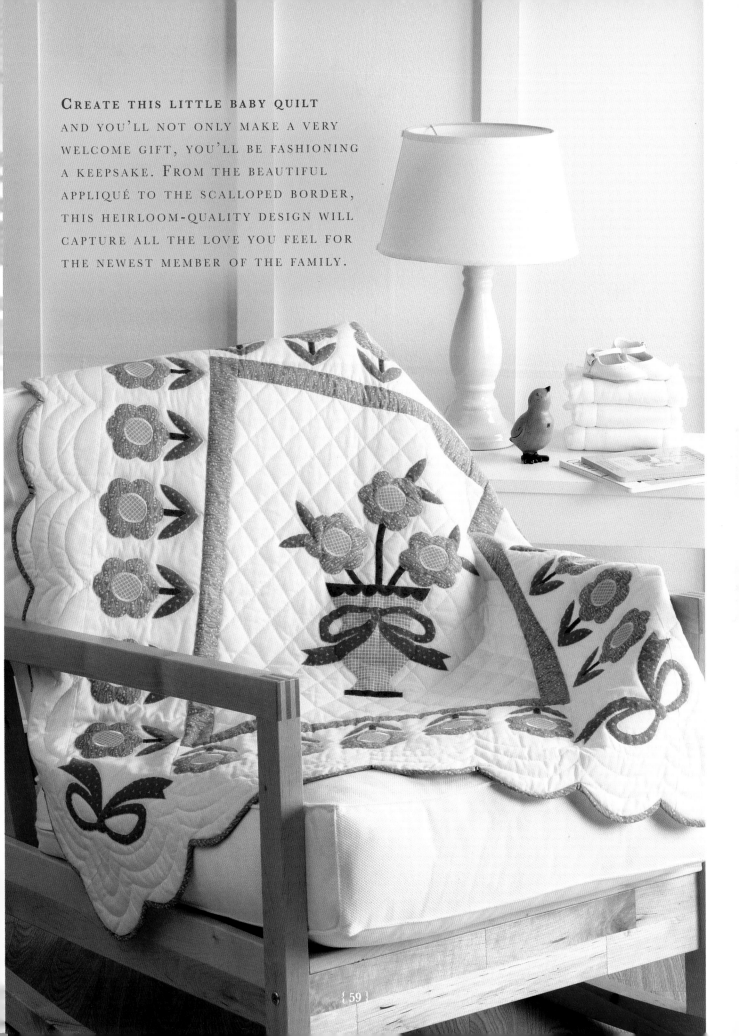

Preparing the Appliqués

*Use patterns, pages 62-63, and follow **Preparing Fusible Appliqués**, page 84, to make appliqués.*
From light blue print fabric:
- Cut 25 **flowers**.

From blue print fabric:
- Cut 25 **leaves**.
- Cut 5 **bows**.

From light blue check fabric:
- Cut 25 **flower centers**.
- Cut 1 **vase**.

From dark blue print fabric:
- Cut 24 **short stems**.
- Cut 1 **long stem**.
- Cut 1 **scallop**.
- Cut 1 **base**.

Assembling the Quilt Top

*Follow **Machine Piecing**, page 81, and **Pressing**, page 83. Use a $^1/_4$" seam allowance.*

1. Reserving **flower centers** and 4 **bows**, refer to **Quilt Top Diagram** and follow **Satin Stitch Appliqué**, page 84, to use technique to arrange and fuse **appliqués** and stitch to **rectangle** and **appliqué panels** using clear monofilament thread, a narrow stitch width, and a short stitch length.

2. Arrange and fuse flower centers to each flower. Stitch 1 flower center to each **flower** appliqué using general-purpose thread, a wide stitch width, and a short stitch length.

3. Trim **rectangle** to $17^1/_2$" x $22^1/_2$". Trim **side appliqué panels** to $6^1/_2$" x $25^1/_2$"; trim **top/ bottom appliqué panels** to $6^1/_2$" x $20^1/_2$".

4. Sew **top, bottom**, then **side inner borders** to **rectangle**.

5. Sew 1 **corner square** to each end of each **side appliqué panel**. Sew **top, bottom**, then **side appliqué panels** to **rectangle** to make center section of quilt top.

6. Sew 1 **corner square** to each end of each **side outer border**. Sew **top, bottom**, then **side outer borders** to center section.

7. Referring to **Quilt Top Diagram**, stitch bows to corners using clear monofilament thread, a narrow stitch width, and a short stitch length.

Completing the Quilt

1. Measure $4^1/_2$" from inner corner of outer border square along each seamline towards outer edges. From these points, measure over 4" toward outer corner of quilt top; mark dots. Repeat for remaining corners. On each side of quilt top, draw a line connecting dots.

2. Beginning at dots, mark dots at 5" intervals along drawn line. Use a compass or round object to draw scalloped lines connecting dots. At corners, connect dots to round corner. Do not trim.

3. Follow **Quilting**, page 87, to mark, layer, and quilt using **Quilting Diagram**, page 62, as a suggestion. Our quilt is hand quilted.

4. Cut a 20" square of binding fabric. Follow **Making Continuous Bias Strip Binding**, page 91, to make $1^5/_8$"w bias binding.

5. Following Steps 1 and 2 of **Attaching Binding with Mitered Corners**, page 92, pin binding to front of quilt, matching raw edges of binding to scalloped line. Using a $1/4"$ seam allowance and easing around curves, sew binding to quilt until binding overlaps beginning end by $2"$; trim excess binding. Trim quilt top, batting, and backing even with raw edges of binding. Fold binding over to quilt backing and pin in place, covering stitching line. Blindstitch binding to backing.

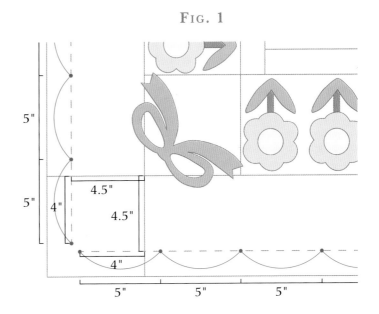

FIG. 1

QUILT TOP DIAGRAM

QUILTING DIAGRAM

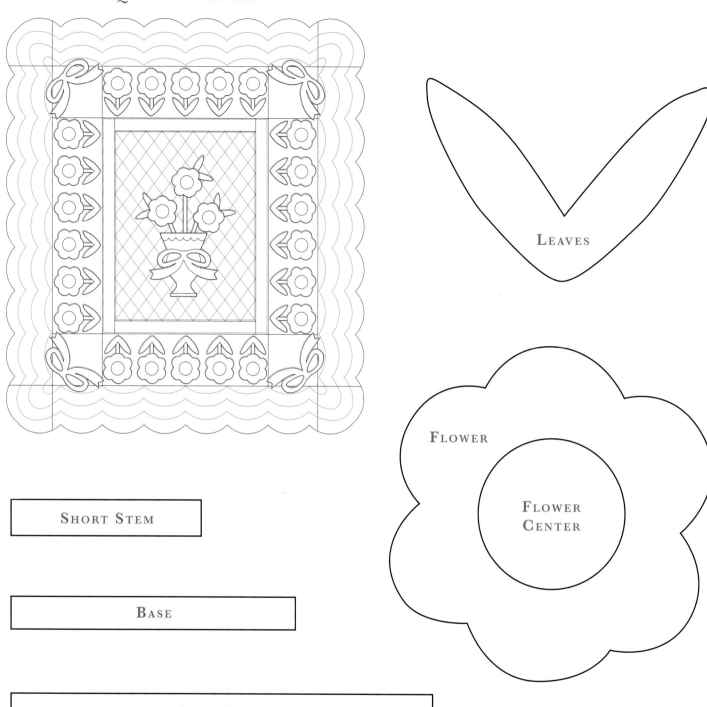

LEAVES

FLOWER

FLOWER CENTER

SHORT STEM

BASE

LONG STEM

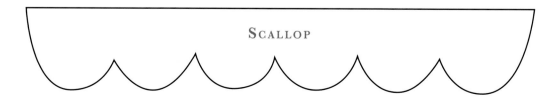

SCALLOP

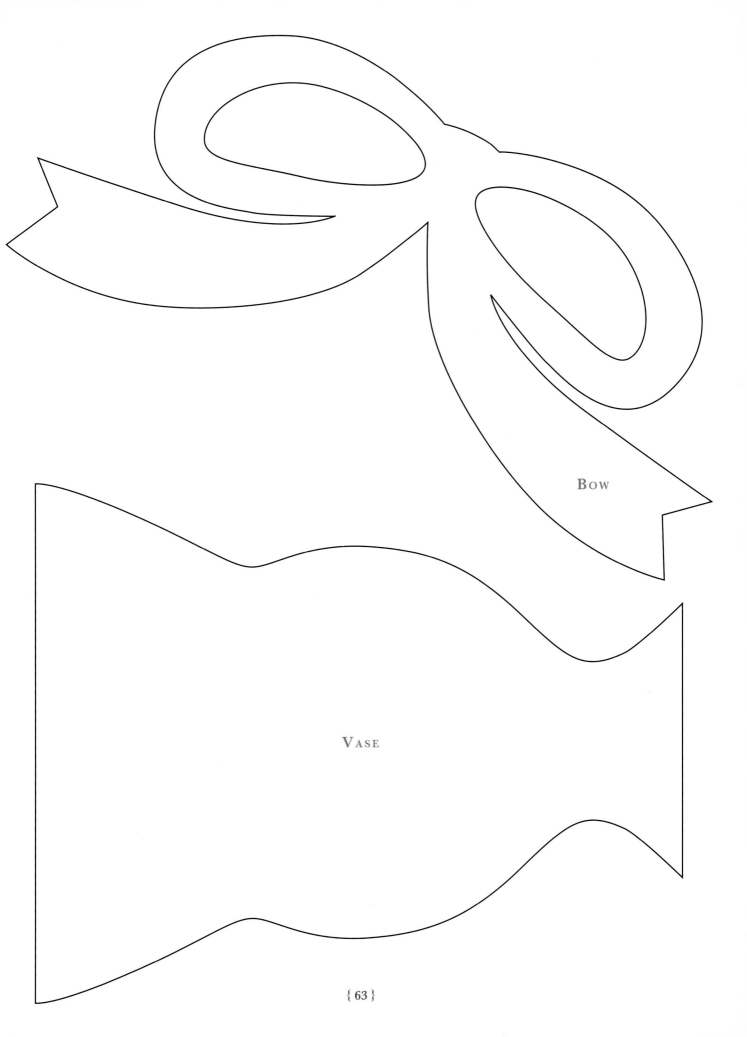

Bow

Vase

Iris
WALL HANGING

FINISHED WALL HANGING SIZE:
$26\frac{1}{2}$" x $26\frac{1}{2}$" (67 CM x 67 CM)

FINISHED BLOCK SIZE:
$6\frac{1}{2}$" x $6\frac{1}{2}$" (17 CM x 17 CM)

Yardage Requirements

Yardage is based on 43"/44" (109 cm/112 cm) wide fabric with a usable width of 40" (102 cm).

$\frac{3}{8}$ yd (34 cm) of blue stripe fabric
$\frac{1}{4}$ yd (23 cm) of white print fabric
$\frac{1}{8}$ yd (11 cm) of purple dot print fabric
Scraps of 4 blue solids, 2 green solids, and
  1 yellow print for appliqués
5" x 13" (13 cm x 33 cm) piece **each** of
  4 dark blue prints
5" x 13" (13 cm x 33 cm) piece **each** of
  4 light blue prints
1 yd (91 cm) of fabric for backing
$\frac{3}{8}$ yd (34 cm) of fabric for binding

You will also need:
  $30\frac{1}{2}$" x $30\frac{1}{2}$" (77 cm x 77 cm) piece
   of batting
  Paper-backed fusible web
  Transparent monofilament thread

THIS WALL HANGING WOULD BE A THOUGHTFUL
GIFT FOR SOMEONE WHO LOVES BEARDED IRISES. THE
PIECED BLOCKS GO TOGETHER QUICKLY, LEAVING ONLY
THE FOUR IRIS BLOCKS TO COMPLETE WITH FUSIBLE
APPLIQUÉ AND MACHINE STITCHING.

Cutting the Pieces

*Follow **Rotary Cutting**, page 80, to cut fabric. Cut all strips across the selvage-to-selvage width of the fabric unless otherwise indicated. All measurements include ¹/₄" seam allowances.*

From blue stripe fabric:
- Cut 5 strips 2"w. From these strips, cut 24 **sashing strips** 2" x 7".

From white print fabric:
- Cut 4 **background squares** 7" x 7".

From purple dot print fabric:
- Cut 1 strip 2"w. From this strip, cut 16 **sashing squares** 2" x 2".

From scraps for appliqués:
- Referring to **Appliquéd Block** diagram, follow **Preparing Fusible Appliqués**, page 84, and use patterns, page 69, to cut 4 **each** of **A - I** (cut 2 of the **H's** and 2 of the **I's** in reverse).

From *each* dark blue print fabric:
- Cut 3 squares 4¹/₈" x 4¹/₈". Cut squares once diagonally to make 6 **dark triangles** (you will need 5 and have 1 left over from each print).

From *each* light blue print fabric:
- Cut 3 squares 4¹/₈" x 4¹/₈". Cut squares once diagonally to make 6 **light triangles** (you will need 5 and have 1 left over from each print).

From fabric for binding:
- Cut 4 **binding strips** 2¹/₂" x 29".

Assembling the Wall Hanging Top

*Follow **Machine Piecing**, page 81, and **Pressing**, page 83. Use a ¹/₄" seam allowance.*

1. Sew 1 **dark triangle** and 1 **light triangle** together to make **triangle-square**. Make 20 triangle-squares.
2. Sew 4 **triangle-squares** together to make **Pieced Block**. Make 5 Pieced Blocks.
3. Follow **Satin Stitch Appliqué**, page 84, to use technique to stitch **appliqués** to **background square** using monofilament thread, a narrow stitch width, and a short stitch length to make **Appliquéd Block**. Make 4 Appliquéd Blocks.
4. Sew 4 **sashing squares** and 3 **sashing strips** together to make **Sashing Row**. Make 4 Sashing Rows.

TRIANGLE-SQUARES
(MAKE 5 OF EACH)

PIECED BLOCK
(MAKE 5)

APPLIQUÉD BLOCK
(MAKE 4)

5. Referring to **Wall Hanging Top Diagram**, sew sashing strips, **Pieced Blocks**, and **Appliquéd Blocks** together to make 3 **Rows**.

6. Sew **Sashing Rows** and **Rows** together to complete **Wall Hanging Top**.

SASHING ROW
(MAKE **4**)

WALL HANGING TOP DIAGRAM

Completing the Wall Hanging

1. Follow **Quilting**, page 87, to mark, layer, and quilt using **Quilting Diagram** as a suggestion. Our wall hanging is hand quilted in the ditch around appliqués and along the seams in the Pieced Block. Parallel wavy lines are quilted in the sashing strips.

2. Follow **Making A Hanging Sleeve**, page 91, to attach hanging sleeve to wall hanging.

3. Matching wrong sides and raw edges, press binding strips in half. Follow **Attaching Binding with Overlapped Corners**, page 93, to attach binding to quilt.

QUILTING DIAGRAM

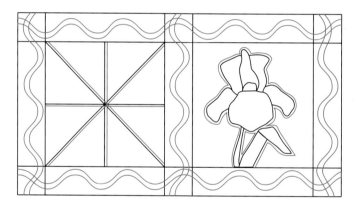

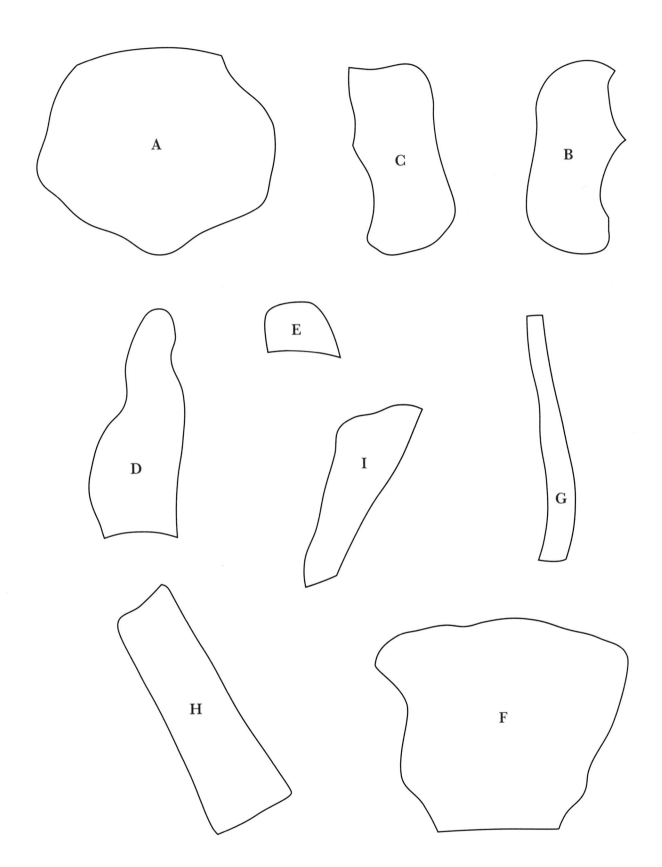

Floral Nine-Patch
QUILT

FINISHED QUILT SIZE:
86" x 98" (218 CM x 249 CM)

FINISHED BLOCK SIZE:
9" x 9" (23 CM x 23 CM)

Yardage Requirements

Yardage is based on 43"/44" (109 cm/112 cm) wide fabric with a usable width of 40" (102 cm).

$4^{1}/_{2}$ yds (4.1 m) of large floral print fabric
$3^{5}/_{8}$ yds (3.3 m) of green print fabric
$3^{1}/_{2}$ yds (3.2 m) of purple print fabric
$1^{3}/_{4}$ yds (1.6 m) of white print fabric
$7^{7}/_{8}$ yds (7.2 m) of fabric for backing
1 yd (91 cm) of fabric for binding

You will also need:

94" x 106" (239 cm x 269 cm) piece of batting

Cutting the Pieces

*Follow **Rotary Cutting**, page 80, to cut fabric. Cut all strips across the selvage-to-selvage width of the fabric unless otherwise indicated. Borders are cut longer than necessary and will be trimmed to fit quilt top center. All measurements include $^{1}/_{4}$" seam allowances.*

From large floral print fabric:
- Cut 15 **wide strips** $3^{1}/_{2}$" wide.
- Cut 4 strips $3^{1}/_{2}$"w. From these strips, cut 42 **sashing squares** $3^{1}/_{2}$" x $3^{1}/_{2}$".
- Cut 2 *lengthwise* **top/bottom wide borders** $8^{1}/_{2}$" x $85^{1}/_{2}$".
- Cut 2 *lengthwise* **side wide borders** $8^{1}/_{2}$" x $81^{1}/_{2}$".

From green print fabric:
- Cut 18 **narrow strips** $1^{1}/_{2}$" wide.
- Cut 2 *lengthwise* **side outer borders** $2^{1}/_{2}$" x $97^{1}/_{2}$".
- Cut 2 *lengthwise* **top/bottom outer borders** $2^{1}/_{2}$" x $89^{1}/_{2}$".

From purple print fabric:
- Cut 12 **wide strips** $3^{1}/_{2}$" wide.
- Cut 2 *lengthwise* **side inner borders** $1^{1}/_{2}$" x $79^{1}/_{2}$".
- Cut 2 *lengthwise* **top/bottom inner borders** $1^{1}/_{2}$" x $69^{1}/_{2}$".

From white print fabric:
- Cut 36 **narrow strips** $1^{1}/_{2}$" wide.

MAKE A BED-SIZE QUILT
THAT'S COVERED IN FLOWERS
YET FINISHED IN A FLASH? YES!
JUST LET A LARGE FLORAL PRINT
PROVIDE ALL THE BLOSSOMS.
NINE-PATCH SQUARES, SIMPLE
SASHING, AND A WIDE BORDER
WILL HELP YOU PUT THIS QUILT
TOP TOGETHER IN NO TIME.

Assembling the Quilt Top

*Follow **Machine Piecing**, page 81, and **Pressing**, page 83. Use a $1/4$" seam allowance.*

1. Sew 2 large floral print **wide strips** and 1 purple print **wide strip** together to make **Strip Set A**. Make 6 Strip Set A's. Cut across Strip Set A's at $3^1/2$" intervals to make 60 **Unit 1's**.

2. Sew 2 purple print **wide strips** and 1 large floral print **wide strip** together to make **Strip Set B**. Make 3 Strip Set B's. Cut across Strip Set B's at $3^1/2$" intervals to make 30 **Unit 2's**.

3. Sew 2 **Unit 1's** and 1 **Unit 2** together to make **Block**. Make 30 Blocks.

4. Sew 2 white print **narrow strips** and 1 green print **narrow strip** together to make **Strip Set C**. Make 18 **Strip Set C's**. Cut across Strip Set C's at $9^1/2$" intervals to make 71 **Sashing Units**.

5. Sew 5 **Blocks** and 6 **Sashing Units** together to make **Row**. Make 6 Rows.

6. Sew 6 **sashing squares** and 5 **Sashing Units** together to make **Sashing Row**. Make 7 Sashing Rows.

7. Referring to **Quilt Top Diagram**, sew **Sashing Rows** and **Rows** together to make center section of quilt top.

8. Follow **Adding Squared Borders**, page 86, to sew **side**, then **top** and **bottom inner borders** to center section. Repeat to add **wide borders**, then **outer borders** to complete **Quilt Top**.

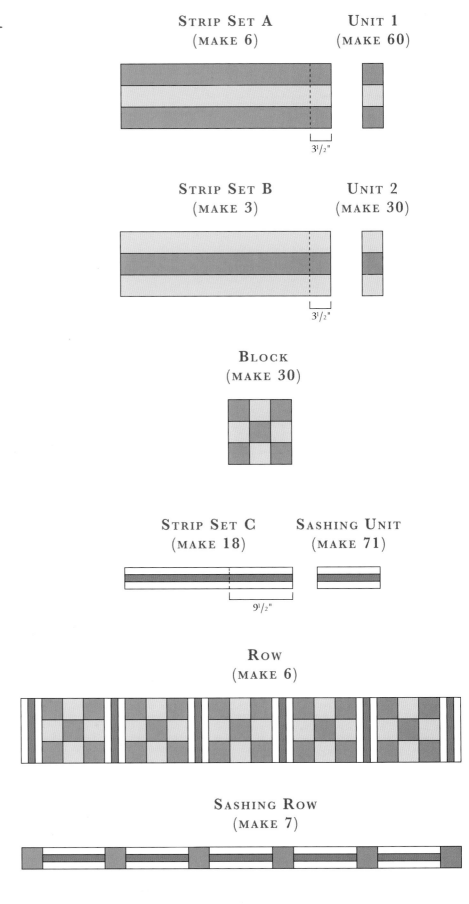

STRIP SET A
(MAKE **6**)

UNIT 1
(MAKE **60**)

$3^1/2$"

STRIP SET B
(MAKE **3**)

UNIT 2
(MAKE **30**)

$3^1/2$"

BLOCK
(MAKE **30**)

STRIP SET C
(MAKE **18**)

SASHING UNIT
(MAKE **71**)

$9^1/2$"

ROW
(MAKE **6**)

SASHING ROW
(MAKE **7**)

Completing the Wall Hanging

1. Follow **Quilting**, page 87, to mark, layer, and quilt using **Quilting Diagram** as a suggestion. Our quilt is hand quilted.

2. Cut a 33" square of binding fabric. Follow **Making Continuous Bias Strip Binding**, page 91, to make $2^1/_2$"w bias binding. Follow **Attaching Binding with Mitered Corners**, page 92, to attach binding to quilt.

QUILTING DIAGRAM

QUILT TOP DIAGRAM

Good Fortune
WALL HANGING

FINISHED WALL HANGING SIZE:
35" x 35" (89 cm x 89 cm)

FINISHED BLOCK SIZE:
4" x 4" (10 cm x 10 cm)

Yardage Requirements

Yardage is based on 43"/44" (109 cm/112 cm) wide fabric with a usable width of 40" (102 cm).

   1 yd (91 cm) of white solid fabric
   1 yd (91 cm) of blue solid fabric
   $^1/_4$ yd (23 cm) of blue print fabric
   Scraps of assorted fabrics for appliqués
   $1^3/_8$ yds (1.3 m) of fabric for backing and
    hanging sleeve
   $^3/_4$ yd (69 cm) of fabric for binding
You will also need:
   39" x 39" (99 cm x 99 cm) piece of batting
   Clear monofilament thread

HIGH COLOR CONTRAST AND PRETTY APPLIQUÉ ADD UP TO REAL BEAUTY ON THIS LITTLE BLUE-AND-WHITE QUILT. THE PIECED BLOCKS ARE THE ESSENCE OF EASINESS— JUST ADD FOUR TRIANGLES TO THE CENTER RECTANGLE! THE CORNER FLOWERS ARE ALSO QUICK TO ADD WITH MACHINE APPLIQUÉ. PERFECTLY SIZED FOR A TABLE TOPPER OR WALL HANGING, THIS DESIGN WILL ADD A FRESH NEW LOOK TO ANY ROOM.

Cutting the Pieces

*Follow **Rotary Cutting**, page 80, to cut fabric. Cut all strips across the selvage-to-selvage width of the fabric unless otherwise indicated. Borders are cut longer than necessary and will be trimmed to fit quilt top center. All measurements include $^1/_4$" seam allowances.*

From white solid fabric:

- Cut 2 strips $4^3/_8$"w. From these strips, cut 21 **rectangles** $2^1/_4$" x $4^3/_8$".
- Cut 2 strips $3^5/_8$"w. From these strips, cut 16 squares $3^5/_8$" x $3^5/_8$". Cut squares once diagonally to make 32 **large triangles**.
- Cut 1 strip $2^1/_8$"w. From this strip, cut 16 squares $2^1/_8$" x $2^1/_8$". Cut squares once diagonally to make 32 **small triangles**.
- Cut 2 strips $4^1/_2$"w. From these strips, cut 12 **squares** $4^1/_2$" x $4^1/_2$".

From blue solid fabric:

- Cut 2 **side outer borders** $2^1/_2$" x $38^1/_2$".
- Cut 2 **top/bottom outer borders** $2^1/_2$" x $34^1/_2$".
- Cut 1 strip $4^3/_8$"w. From this strip, cut 16 **rectangles** $2^1/_4$" x $4^3/_8$".
- Cut 2 strips $3^5/_8$"w. From these strips, cut 21 squares $3^5/_8$" x $3^5/_8$". Cut each square once diagonally to make 42 **large triangles**.
- Cut 2 strips $2^1/_8$"w. From these strips, cut 21 squares $2^1/_8$" x $2^1/_8$". Cut each square once diagonally to make 42 **small triangles**.

From blue print fabric:

- Cut 2 **side inner borders** $1^1/_2$" x $34^1/_2$".
- Cut 2 **top/bottom inner borders** $1^1/_2$" x $32^1/_2$".

From remaining fabrics and scraps:

- Referring to **Wall Hanging Top Diagram**, page 78, use patterns, page 79, and follow **Preparing Fusible Appliqués**, page 84, to make 12 **flower**, 12 **flower center**, and 4 **corner trim** appliqués.

Assembling the Wall Hanging Top

*Follow **Machine Piecing**, page 81, and **Pressing**, page 83. Use a $^1/_4$" seam allowance.*

1. Sew 2 blue solid **small triangles** and 1 white solid **rectangle** together to make **Unit 1a**. Make 21 Unit 1a's. Sew 2 white solid **small triangles** and 1 blue solid **rectangle** together to make **Unit 1b**. Make 16 Unit 1b's.

UNIT 1A
(MAKE 21)

UNIT 1B
(MAKE 16)

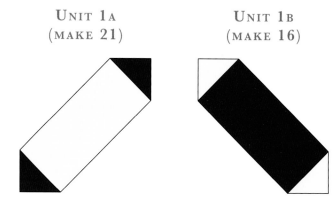

2. Sew 2 blue solid **large triangles** and 1 **Unit 1a** together to make **Unit 2a**. Make 21 Unit 2a's. Sew 2 white solid **large triangles** and 1 **Unit 1b** together to make **Unit 2b**. Make 16 Unit 2b's.

3. Sew 4 white solid **squares**, 2 **Unit 2a's**, and 1 **Unit 2b** together to make **Row A**. Make 2 Row A's. Sew 2 white solid **squares**, 3 **Unit 2a's**, and 2 **Unit 2b's** together to make **Row B**. Make 2 Row B's. Sew 4 **Unit 2a's** and 3 **Unit 2b's** together to make **Row C**. Make 2 Row C's. Sew 4 **Unit 2b's** and 3 **Unit 2a's** together to make 1 **Row D**.

UNIT 2A
(MAKE 21)

UNIT 2B
(MAKE 16)

ROW A
(MAKE 2)

ROW B
(MAKE 2)

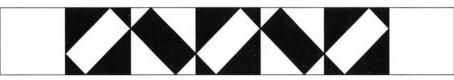

ROW C
(MAKE 2)

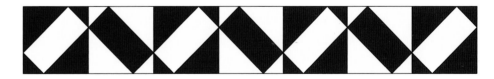

ROW D
(MAKE 1)

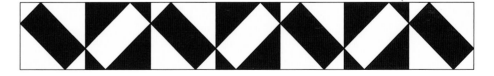

4. Referring to **Wall Hanging Top Diagram**, sew **Rows** together to make center section of wall hanging top.

5. Follow **Adding Squared Borders**, page 86, to sew **top, bottom**, then **side inner borders** to center section of wall hanging top. Repeat to add **outer borders** to center section of wall hanging top.

6. Follow **Satin Stitch Appliqué**, page 84, to use technique to stitch appliqués to wall hanging using monofilament thread, a narrow stitch width, and a short stitch length to complete **Wall Hanging Top**.

Completing the Wall Hanging

1. Follow **Quilting**, page 87, to mark, layer, and quilt using **Quilting Diagram** as a suggestion. Our quilt is hand quilted.

2. Follow **Making a Hanging Sleeve**, page 91, to attach hanging sleeve to wall hanging.

3. Cut a 22" square of binding fabric. Follow **Making Continuous Bias Strip Binding**, page 91, to make 2¹/₂"w bias binding. Follow **Attaching Binding with Mitered Corners**, page 92, to attach binding to quilt.

WALL HANGING TOP DIAGRAM

QUILTING DIAGRAM

CORNER TRIM

FLOWER
CENTER

FLOWER

{ 79 }

General
INSTRUCTIONS

To make your quilting easier and more enjoyable, we encourage you to carefully read all of the general instructions, study the color photographs, and familiarize yourself with the individual project instructions before beginning a project.

Fabrics

SELECTING FABRICS
Choose high-quality, medium-weight 100% cotton fabrics. All-cotton fabrics hold a crease better, fray less, and are easier to quilt than cotton/polyester blends.

Yardage requirements listed for each project are based on 43"/44" wide fabric with a "usable" width of 40" after shrinkage and trimming selvages. Actual usable width will probably vary slightly from fabric to fabric. Our recommended yardage lengths should be adequate for occasional re-squaring of fabric when many cuts are required.

PREPARING FABRICS
We recommend that all fabrics be washed, dried, and pressed before cutting. If fabrics are not pre-washed, washing the finished quilt will cause shrinkage and give it a more "antiqued" look and feel. Bright and dark colors, which may run, should always be washed before cutting. After washing and drying fabric, fold lengthwise with wrong sides together and matching selvages.

Rotary Cutting
Rotary cutting has brought speed and accuracy to quiltmaking by allowing quilters to easily cut strips of fabric and then cut those strips into smaller pieces.

- Place fabric on work surface with fold closest to you.

- Cut all strips from the selvage-to-selvage width of the fabric unless otherwise indicated in project instructions.

- Square left edge of fabric using rotary cutter and rulers (**Figs. 1 - 2**).

- To cut each strip required for a project, place ruler over cut edge of fabric, aligning desired marking on ruler with cut edge; make cut (**Fig. 3**).

- When cutting several strips from a single piece of fabric, it is important to make sure that cuts remain at a perfect right angle to the fold; square fabric as needed.

FIG. 1

FIG. 2

FIG. 3

Template Cutting

Our piecing template patterns have two lines – a solid cutting line and a dashed line showing the ¹/₄" seam allowance. (Patterns for appliqué templates do not include seam allowances.)

1. To make a template from a pattern, use a permanent fine-point pen and a ruler to carefully trace pattern onto template plastic, making sure to transfer any alignment and grainline markings. Cut out template along inner edge of drawn line. Check template against original pattern for accuracy.

2. To use a template, place template face down on wrong side of fabric (unless otherwise indicated in project instructions), aligning grainline on template with straight grain of fabric. Use a sharp fabric-marking pencil to draw around template. Transfer all alignment markings to fabric. Cut out fabric piece using scissors or rotary cutting equipment.

Piecing

Precise cutting, followed by accurate piecing, will ensure that all pieces of quilt top fit together well.

HAND PIECING

- Use ruler and sharp fabric marking pencil to draw all seam lines and transfer any alignment markings onto back of cut pieces.

- Matching right sides, pin two pieces together, using pins to mark corners.

- Use a Running Stitch to sew pieces together along drawn line, backstitching at beginning and end of seam.

- Do not extend stitches into seam allowances.

- Run five or six stitches onto needle before pulling needle through fabric.

- To add stability, backstitch every ³/₄" to 1".

MACHINE PIECING

- Set sewing machine stitch length for approximately 11 stitches per inch.

- Use neutral-colored general-purpose sewing thread (not quilting thread) in needle and in bobbin.

- An accurate ¹/₄" seam allowance is *essential*. Presser feet that are ¹/₄" wide are available for most sewing machines.

- When piecing, always place pieces right sides together and match raw edges; pin if necessary.

- Chain piecing saves time and will usually result in more accurate piecing.

- Trim away points of seam allowances that extend beyond edges of sewn pieces.

Sewing Strip Sets

When there are several strips to assemble into a strip set, first sew strips together into pairs, then sew pairs together to form strip set. To help avoid distortion, sew seams in opposite directions (**Fig. 4**).

Sewing Across Seam Intersections

When sewing across intersection of two seams, place pieces right sides together and match seams exactly, making sure seam allowances are pressed in opposite directions (**Fig. 5**).

Sewing Sharp Points

To ensure sharp points when joining triangular or diagonal pieces, stitch across the center of the "X" (shown in pink) formed on wrong side by previous seams (**Fig. 6**).

FOUNDATION PIECING

Preparing Your Sewing Machine

1. To prepare your sewing machine for foundation piecing, insert a 90/14 needle.
2. Set your machine to a short straight stitch (18 stitches per inch). It is helpful to use an open-toe foot.

Piecing

1. Place your original pattern nearby as a guide.
2. Thread your machine with a neutral-colored thread.
3. Rough cut a piece of fabric at least $1/2$" larger on all sides than area 1 on the foundation.
4. Center fabric piece right side up on back of foundation; completely cover area 1 with fabric.
5. Fold foundation on line between area 1 and area 2. Trim fabric $1/4$" from fold (**Fig. 7**). Unfold foundation.
6. Rough cut a piece of fabric in the same manner for area 2 on foundation. Matching trimmed edge, place piece #2 right sides together on piece #1, making sure fabric extends beyond outer seamlines (**Fig. 8**). Turn foundation over to front and pin.
7. Sew along line between areas 1 and 2, extending sewing a few stitches beyond beginning and end of line (**Fig. 9**).
8. Open out piece #2; press. Pin piece #2 to foundation (**Fig. 10**).
9. Repeat adding pieces in same manner until foundation is covered.
10. Trim fabric and foundation $1/4$" beyond outer lines.
11. Sew paper pieced sections together along outer lines; remove paper.

FIG. 4

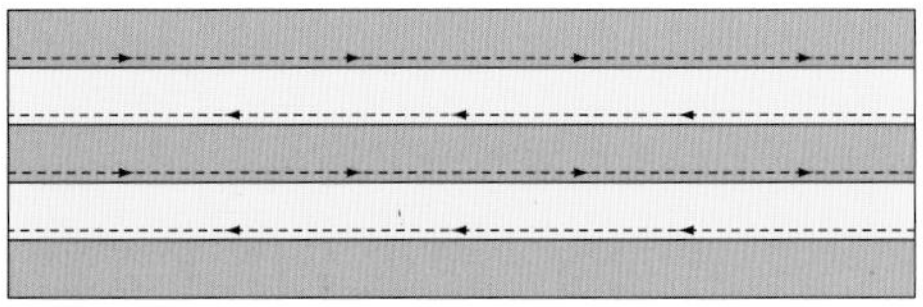

FIG. 5

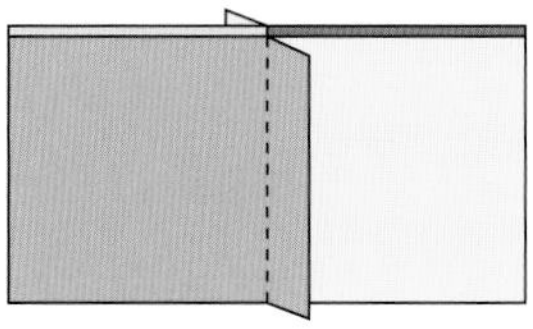

FIG. 6

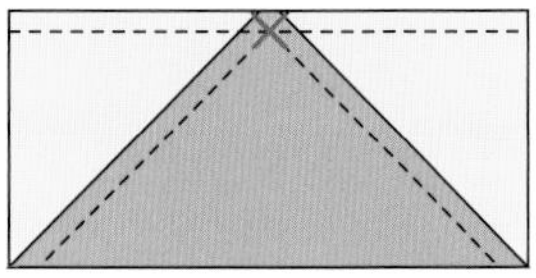

FIG. 7

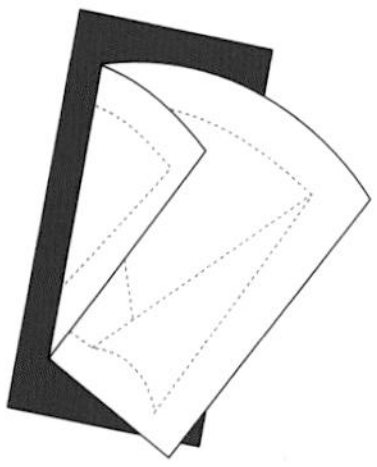

FIG. 8

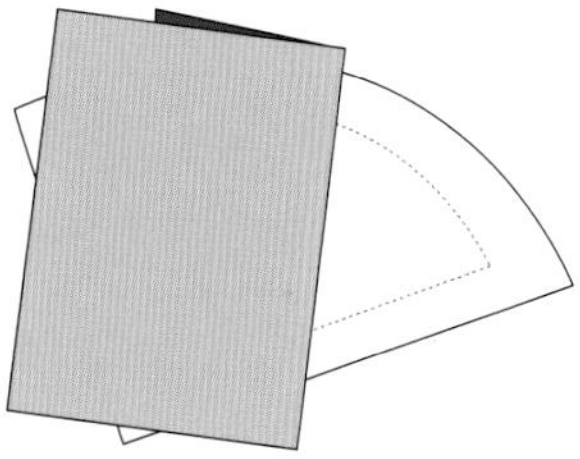

FIG. 9

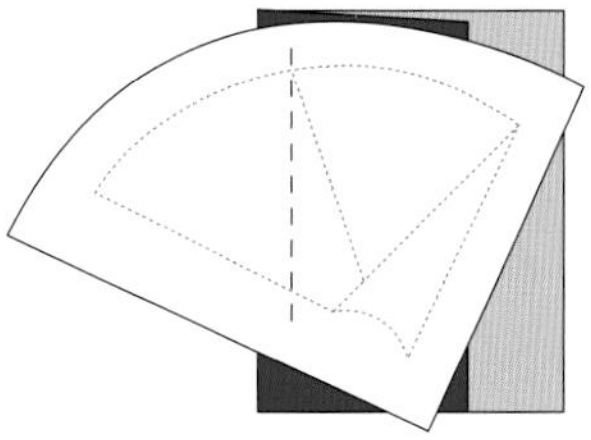

FIG. 10

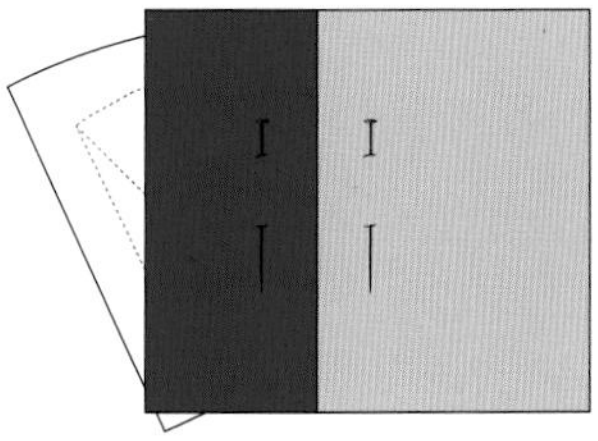

Pressing

- Use steam iron set on "Cotton" for all pressing.

- Press after sewing each seam.

- Seam allowances are almost always pressed to one side, usually toward darker fabric. However, to reduce bulk it may occasionally be necessary to press seam allowances toward the lighter fabric or even to press them open.

- To prevent dark fabric seam allowance from showing through light fabric, trim darker seam allowance slightly narrower than lighter seam allowance.

- To press long seams, such as those in long strip sets, without curving or other distortion, lay strips across width of the ironing board.

Appliqué

NEEDLE-TURN APPLIQUÉ
Using needle to turn under seam allowance while blindstitching appliqué to background fabric is called "needle-turn appliqué."

1. Place template on right side of appliqué fabric. Lightly draw around template with pencil, leaving at least $1/2$" between shapes. Repeat for number of shapes specified in project instructions.
2. Cut out shapes approximately $3/16$" outside drawn line. Clip inside curves and points to, but not through, drawn line. Arrange shapes on background fabric and pin or baste in place.
3. Thread a sharps needle with a single strand of general-purpose sewing thread that matches appliqué; knot one end.
4. Begin blindstitching on as straight an edge as possible, turning a small section of seam allowance to wrong side with needle, concealing drawn line (**Fig. 11**).
5. To stitch outward points, stitch to $1/2$" from point (**Fig. 12**). Turn seam allowance under at point (**Fig. 13**); then turn remainder of seam allowance between stitching and point. Stitch to point, taking two or three stitches at top of point to secure. Turn under small amount of seam allowance past point and resume stitching.
6. To stitch inward point, stitch to $1/2$" from point (**Fig. 14**). Clip to but not through seam allowance at point (**Fig. 15**). Turn seam allowance under between stitching and point. Stitch to point, taking two or three stitches at point to secure. Turn under small amount of seam allowance past point and resume stitching.

FIG. 11	FIG. 12	FIG. 13	FIG. 14	FIG. 15

7. Do not turn under or stitch seam allowances that will be covered by other appliqué pieces.

8. To appliqué pressed bias strips, baste strips in place and blindstitch along edges.

9. To reduce bulk, background fabric behind appliqués may be cut away. After stitching appliqués in place, turn block over and use sharp scissors or specially designed appliqué scissors to trim away background fabric approximately $3/16$" from stitching line. Take care not to cut appliqué fabric or stitches.

MACHINE APPLIQUÉ

Preparing Fusible Appliqués

Patterns are printed in reverse to enable you to use our speedy method of preparing appliqués. White or light-colored fabrics may need to be lined with fusible interfacing before applying fusible web to prevent darker fabrics from showing through.

1. Place paper-backed fusible web, paper side up, over appliqué pattern. Trace pattern onto paper side of web with pencil as many times as indicated in project instructions for a single fabric.

2. Follow manufacturer's instructions to fuse traced patterns to wrong side of fabrics. Do not remove paper backing. (*Note:* Some pieces may be given as measurements, such as a 2" x 4" rectangle, instead of drawn patterns. Fuse web to wrong side of fabrics indicated for these pieces.)

3. Use scissors to cut out appliqué pieces along traced lines; use rotary cutting equipment to cut out appliqué pieces given as measurements. Remove paper backing from all pieces.

4. Arrange appliqué pieces on background; fuse in place.

Satin Stitch Appliqué

This machine appliqué method can be done using general-purpose sewing thread or clear monofilament thread. Monofilament thread is available in clear and smoke. Use clear on white or very light fabrics and smoke on darker colors. While these instructions are written for a medium stitch width and a short stitch to make a thick, smooth, almost solid line of zigzag stitching, the same techniques apply when using a zigzag stitch with a shorter or longer stitch length.

1. Pin stabilizer, such as paper or any of the commercially available products, on wrong side of background fabric before stitching appliqués in place.

2. Thread sewing machine with general-purpose thread or clear monofilament thread; use general-purpose thread that matches background fabric in bobbin.

3. Set sewing machine for a medium (approximately $1/8$") stitch width and a short stitch length for a thick, smooth, almost solid line of stitching. Set machine for a medium stitch width and a longer stitch length for a zigzag stitch. Slightly loosening the top tension may yield a smoother stitch.

4. Begin by stitching two or three stitches in place (drop feed dogs or set stitch length at 0) to anchor thread. Most of the Satin Stitch should be on the appliqué with the right edge of the stitch falling at the outside edge of the appliqué. Stitch over all exposed raw edges of appliqué pieces.

5. (*Note:* Dots on **Figs. 16 – 21** indicate where to leave needle in fabric when pivoting.) For outside corners, stitch just past corner, stopping with needle in background fabric (**Fig. 16**). Raise presser foot. Pivot project, lower presser foot, and stitch adjacent side (**Fig. 17**).

6. For inside corners, stitch just past corner, stopping with needle in appliqué fabric (**Fig. 18**). Raise presser foot. Pivot project, lower presser foot, and stitch adjacent side (**Fig. 19**).

7. When stitching outside curves, stop with needle in background fabric. Raise presser foot and pivot project as needed. Lower presser foot and continue stitching, pivoting as often as necessary to follow curve (**Fig. 20**).

8. When stitching inside curves, stop with needle in appliqué fabric. Raise presser foot and pivot project as needed. Lower presser foot and continue stitching, pivoting as often as necessary to follow curve (**Fig. 21**).

9. Do not backstitch at end of stitching. Pull threads to wrong side of background fabric; knot thread and trim ends.

10. Carefully tear away stabilizer.

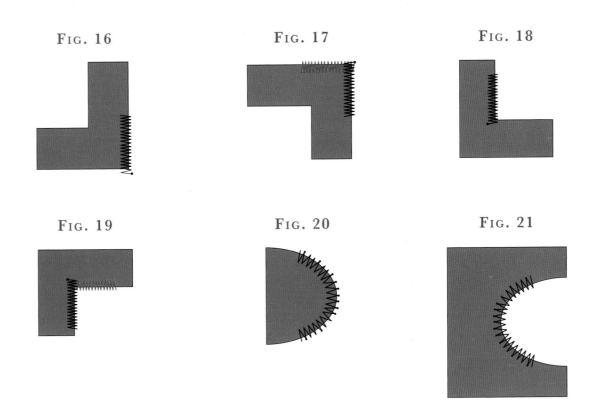

FIG. 16   FIG. 17   FIG. 18

FIG. 19   FIG. 20   FIG. 21

Borders

ADDING SQUARED BORDERS

In most cases, our instructions for cutting borders for bed-size quilts include an extra 2" of length at each end for "insurance;" borders will be trimmed after measuring completed center section of quilt top.

1. Mark the center of each edge of quilt top.
2. Squared borders are usually added to top and bottom, then side edges of the center section of the quilt top. To add top and bottom borders, measure across center of quilt top to determine length of borders (**Fig. 22**). Trim top and bottom borders to the determined length.
3. Mark center of 1 long edge of top border. Matching center marks and raw edges, pin border to quilt top, easing in any fullness; stitch. Repeat for bottom border.
4. Measure center of quilt top, including attached borders, to determine length of side borders. Trim side borders to the determined length. Repeat Step 3 to add borders to quilt top (**Fig. 23**).

ADDING MITERED BORDERS

1. Mark the center of each edge of quilt top.
2. Mark center of 1 long edge of top border. Measure across center of quilt top (see **Fig. 22**). Matching center marks and raw edges, pin border to center of quilt top edge. Beginning at center of border, measure $1/2$ the width of the quilt top in both directions and mark. Match marks on border with corners of quilt top and pin. Easing in any fullness, pin border to quilt top between center and corners. Sew border to quilt top, beginning and ending seams exactly $1/4$" from each corner of quilt top and backstitching at beginning and end of stitching (**Fig. 24**).
3. Repeat Step 2 to sew bottom, then side borders, to center section of quilt top. To temporarily move first 2 borders out of the way, fold and pin ends as shown in **Fig. 25**.
4. Fold 1 corner of quilt top diagonally with right sides together and matching edges. Use ruler to mark stitching line as shown in **Fig. 26**. Pin borders together along drawn line. Sew on drawn line, backstitching at beginning and end of stitching (**Fig. 27**).
5. Turn mitered corner right side up. Check to make sure corner will lie flat with no gaps or puckers.
6. Trim seam allowances to $1/4$"; press to 1 side.
7. Repeat Steps 4-6 to miter each remaining corner.

FIG. 22

FIG. 23

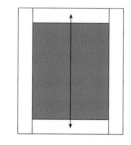

FIG. 24

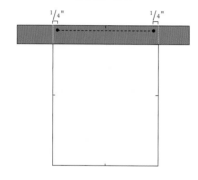

FIG. 25

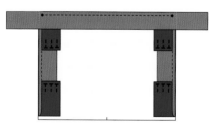

FIG. 26

FIG. 27

Quilting

*Quilting holds the three layers (top, batting, and backing) of the quilt together and can be done by hand or machine. Because marking, layering, and quilting are interrelated and may be done in different orders depending on circumstances, please read entire **Quilting** section, pages 87 – 90, before beginning project.*

TYPES OF QUILTING DESIGNS

In the Ditch Quilting

Quilting along seamlines or along edges of appliquéd pieces is called "in the ditch" quilting. This type of quilting should be done on side **opposite** seam allowance and does not have to be marked.

Outline Quilting

Quilting a consistent distance, usually $1/4$", from seam or appliqué is called "outline" quilting. Outline quilting may be marked, or $1/4$" masking tape may be placed along seamlines for quilting guide. (Do not leave tape on quilt longer than necessary, since it may leave an adhesive residue.)

Motif Quilting

Quilting a design, such as a feathered wreath, is called "motif" quilting. This type of quilting should be marked before basting quilt layers together.

Echo Quilting

Quilting that follows the outline of an appliquéd or pieced design with two or more parallel lines is called "echo" quilting. This type of quilting does not need to be marked.

Channel Quilting

Quilting with straight, parallel lines is called "channel" quilting. This type of quilting may be marked or stitched using a guide.

Crosshatch Quilting

Quilting straight lines in a grid pattern is called "crosshatch" quilting. Lines may be stitched parallel to edges of quilt or stitched diagonally. This type of quilting may be marked or stitched using a guide.

Meandering Quilting

Quilting in random curved lines and swirls is called "meandering" quilting. Quilting lines should not cross or touch each other. This type of quilting does not need to be marked.

Stipple Quilting

Meandering quilting that is very closely spaced is called "stipple" quilting. Stippling will flatten the area quilted and is often stitched in background areas to raise appliquéd or pieced designs. This type of quilting does not need to be marked.

MARKING QUILTING LINES

Quilting lines may be marked using fabric marking pencils, chalk markers or water- or air-soluble pens.

Simple quilting designs may be marked with chalk or chalk pencil after basting. A small area may be marked, then quilted, before moving to next area to be marked. Intricate designs should be marked before basting using a more durable marker.

Caution: Pressing may permanently set some marks. **Test** different markers **on scrap fabric** to find one that marks clearly and can be thoroughly removed.

A wide variety of pre-cut quilting stencils, as well as entire books of quilting patterns, are available. Using a stencil makes it easier to mark intricate or repetitive designs.

To make a stencil from a pattern, center template plastic over pattern and use a permanent marker to trace pattern onto plastic. Use a craft knife with single or double blade to cut channels along traced lines (**Fig. 28**).

FIG. 28

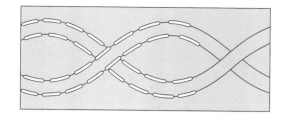

PREPARING THE BACKING

To allow for slight shifting of quilt top during quilting, backing should be approximately 4" larger on all sides for quilts and 2" larger on all sides for wall hangings. Yardage requirements listed for quilt backings are calculated for 43"/44"w fabric. Using 90"w or 108"w fabric for the backing of a bed-sized quilt may eliminate piecing. To piece a backing using 43"/44"w fabric, use the following instructions.

FIG. 29

1. Measure length and width of quilt top; add 8" to each measurement.
2. If determined width is 79" or less, cut backing fabric into two lengths slightly longer than determined *length* measurement. Trim selvages. Place lengths with right sides facing and sew long edges together, forming tube (**Fig. 29**). Match seams and press along one fold (**Fig. 30**). Cut along pressed fold to form single piece (**Fig. 31**).

FIG. 30

3. If determined width is more than 79", it may require less fabric yardage if the backing is pieced horizontally. Divide determined *length* measurement by 40" to determine how many widths will be needed. Cut required number of widths the determined *width* measurement. Trim selvages. Sew long edges together to form single piece.

FIG. 31

4. Trim backing to size determined in Step 1; press seam allowances open.

CHOOSING THE BATTING

The appropriate batting will make quilting easier. For fine hand quilting, choose low-loft batting. All cotton or cotton/polyester blend battings work well for machine quilting because the cotton helps "grip" quilt layers. If quilt is to be tied, a high-loft batting, sometimes called extra-loft or fat batting, may be used to make quilt "fluffy."

Types of batting include cotton, polyester, wool, cotton/polyester blend, cotton/wool blend, and silk.

When selecting batting, refer to package labels for characteristics and care instructions. Cut batting same size as prepared backing.

ASSEMBLING THE QUILT

1. Examine wrong side of quilt top closely; trim any seam allowances and clip any threads that may show through front of the quilt. Press quilt top, being careful not to "set" any marked quilting lines.
2. Place backing *wrong* side up on flat surface. Use masking tape to tape edges of backing to surface. Place batting on top of backing fabric. Smooth batting gently, being careful not to stretch or tear. Center quilt top *right* side up on batting.
3. If hand quilting, begin in center and work toward outer edges to hand baste all layers together. Use long stitches and place basting lines approximately 4" apart (**Fig. 32**). Smooth fullness or wrinkles toward outer edges.

4. If machine quilting, use 1" rustproof safety pins to "pin-baste" all layers together, spacing pins approximately 4" apart. Begin at center and work toward outer edges to secure all layers. If possible, place pins away from areas that will be quilted, although pins may be removed as needed when quilting.

HAND QUILTING

The quilting stitch is a basic running stitch that forms a broken line on quilt top and backing. Stitches on quilt top and backing should be straight and equal in length.

1. Secure center of quilt in hoop or frame. Check quilt top and backing to make sure they are smooth. To help prevent puckers, always begin quilting in the center of quilt and work toward outside edges.
2. Thread needle with 18" - 20" length of quilting thread; knot one end. Using thimble, insert needle into quilt top and batting approximately $^1/_2$" from quilting line. Bring needle up on quilting line (**Fig. 33**); when knot catches on quilt top, give thread a quick, short pull to "pop" knot through fabric into batting (**Fig. 34**).

FIG. 32

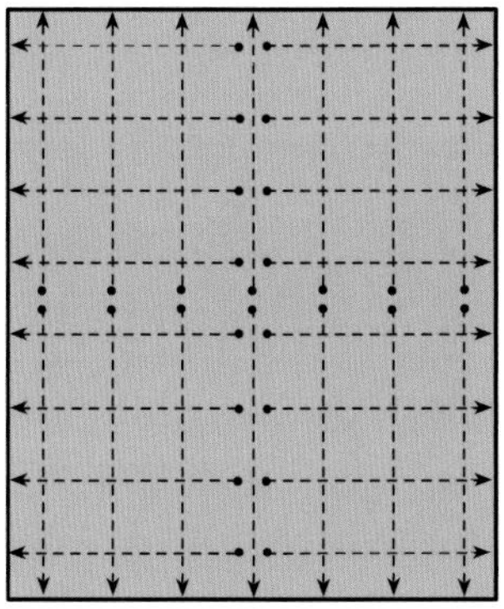

FIG. 33

FIG. 34

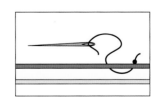

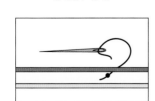

3. Holding needle with sewing hand and placing other hand underneath quilt, use thimble to push tip of needle down through all layers. As soon as needle touches finger underneath, use that finger to push tip of needle only back up through layers to top of quilt. (The amount of needle showing above fabric determines length of quilting stitch.) Referring to **Fig. 35**, rock needle up and down, taking three to six stitches before bringing needle and thread completely through layers. Check back of quilt to make sure stitches are going through all layers. If necessary, make one stitch at a time when quilting through seam allowances or along curves and corners.

4. At end of thread, knot thread close to fabric and "pop" knot into batting; clip thread close to fabric.

5. Move hoop as often as necessary. Thread may be left dangling and picked up again after returning to that part of quilt.

FIG. 35

MACHINE QUILTING METHODS

Use general-purpose thread in bobbin. Do not use quilting thread. Thread the needle of machine with general-purpose thread or transparent monofilament thread to make quilting blend with quilt top fabrics. Use decorative thread, such as a metallic or contrasting-color general-purpose thread, to make quilting lines stand out more.

Straight-Line Quilting
The term "straight-line" is somewhat deceptive, since curves (especially gentle ones) as well as straight lines can be stitched with this technique.

1. Set stitch length for six to ten stitches per inch and attach walking foot to sewing machine.

2. Determine which section of quilt will have longest continuous quilting line, oftentimes area from center top to center bottom. Roll up and secure each edge of quilt to help reduce the bulk, keeping fabrics smooth. Smaller projects may not need to be rolled.

3. Begin stitching on longest quilting line, using very short stitches for the first 1/4" to "lock" quilting. Stitch across project, using one hand on each side of walking foot to slightly spread fabric and to guide fabric through machine. Lock stitches at end of quilting line.

4. Continue machine quilting, stitching longer quilting lines first to stabilize quilt before moving on to other areas.

Free-Motion Quilting
Free-motion quilting may be free form or may follow a marked pattern.

1. Attach darning foot to sewing machine and lower or cover feed dogs.

2. Position quilt under darning foot; lower foot. Holding top thread, take a stitch and pull bobbin thread to top of quilt. To "lock" beginning of quilting line, hold top and bobbin threads while making three to five stitches in place.

3. Use one hand on each side of darning foot to slightly spread fabric and to move fabric through the machine. Even stitch length is achieved by using smooth, flowing hand motion and steady machine speed. Slow machine speed and fast hand movement will create long stitches. Fast machine speed and slow hand movement will create short stitches. Move quilt sideways, back and forth, in a circular motion, or in a random motion to create desired designs; do not rotate quilt. Lock stitches at end of each quilting line.

Making A Hanging Sleeve

Attaching a hanging sleeve to back of wall hanging or quilt before the binding is added allows project to be displayed on wall.

1. Measure width of quilt top edge and subtract 1". Cut piece of fabric 7"w by determined measurement.
2. Press short edges of fabric piece ¼" to wrong side; press edges ¼" to wrong side again and machine stitch in place.
3. Matching wrong sides, fold piece in half lengthwise to form tube.
4. Follow project instructions to sew binding to quilt top and to trim backing and batting. Before Blindstitching binding to backing, match raw edges and stitch hanging sleeve to center top edge on back of quilt.
5. Finish binding quilt, treating hanging sleeve as part of backing.
6. Blindstitch bottom of hanging sleeve to backing, taking care not to stitch through to front of quilt.
7. Insert dowel or slat into hanging sleeve.

Binding

Binding encloses the raw edges of quilt. Because of its stretchiness, bias binding works well for binding projects with curves or rounded corners and tends to lie smooth and flat in any given circumstance. Binding may also be cut from straight lengthwise or crosswise grain of fabric.

MAKING CONTINUOUS BIAS STRIP BINDING

Bias strips for binding can simply be cut and pieced to desired length. However, when a long length of binding is needed, the "continuous" method is quick and accurate.

1. Cut square from binding fabric the size indicated in project instructions. Cut square in half diagonally to make two triangles.
2. With right sides together and using ¼" seam allowance, sew triangles together (**Fig. 36**); press seam allowances open.
3. On wrong side of fabric, draw lines the width of the binding as specified in project instructions, usually 2¹/₂" (**Fig. 37**). Cut off any remaining fabric less than this width.
4. With right sides inside, bring short edges together to form tube; match raw edges so that first drawn line of top section meets second drawn line of bottom section (**Fig. 38**).
5. Carefully pin edges together by inserting pins through drawn lines at point where drawn lines intersect, making sure pins go through intersections on both sides. Using ¼" seam allowance, sew edges together; press seam allowances open.
6. To cut continuous strip, begin cutting along first drawn line (**Fig. 39**). Continue cutting along drawn line around tube.
7. Trim ends of bias strip square.
8. Matching wrong sides and raw edges, carefully press bias strip in half lengthwise to complete binding.

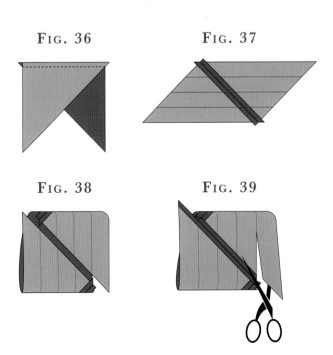

FIG. 36   FIG. 37

FIG. 38   FIG. 39

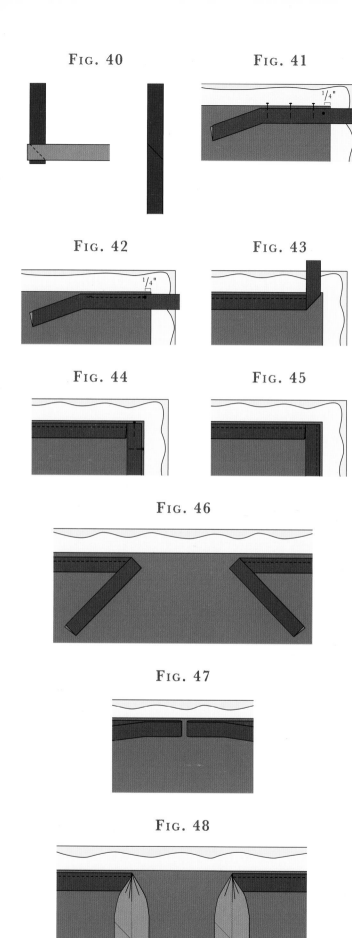

FIG. 40

FIG. 41

FIG. 42

FIG. 43

FIG. 44

FIG. 45

FIG. 46

FIG. 47

FIG. 48

MAKING STRAIGHT-GRAIN BINDING

1. Using diagonal seams (**Fig. 40**), sew binding strips together end to end to make 1 continuous binding strip.
2. Matching wrong sides and raw edges, press strip in half lengthwise.

ATTACHING BINDING WITH MITERED CORNERS

1. Beginning with one end near center on bottom edge of quilt, lay binding around quilt to make sure that seams in binding will not end up at a corner. Adjust placement if necessary. Matching raw edges of binding to raw edge of quilt top, pin binding to right side of quilt along one edge.
2. When you reach first corner, mark $^{1}/_{4}$" from corner of quilt top (**Fig. 41**).
3. Beginning approximately 10" from end of binding and using $^{1}/_{4}$" seam allowance, sew binding to quilt, backstitching at beginning of stitching and at mark (**Fig. 42**). Lift needle out of fabric and clip thread.
4. Fold binding as shown in **Figs. 43 – 44** and pin binding to adjacent side, matching raw edges. When you've reached the next corner, mark $^{1}/_{4}$" from edge of quilt top.
5. Backstitching at edge of quilt top, sew pinned binding to quilt (**Fig. 45**); backstitch at the next mark. Lift needle out of fabric and clip thread.
6. Continue sewing binding to quilt, stopping approximately 10" from starting point (**Fig. 46**).
7. Bring beginning and end of binding to center of opening and fold each end back, leaving a $^{1}/_{4}$" space between folds (**Fig. 47**). Finger press folds.
8. Unfold ends of binding and draw a line across wrong side in finger-pressed crease. Draw a line through the lengthwise pressed fold of binding at the same spot to create a cross mark. With edge of ruler at cross mark, line up 45° angle marking on ruler with one long side of binding. Draw a diagonal line from edge to edge. Repeat on remaining end, making sure that the two diagonal lines are angled the same way (**Fig. 48**).

9. Matching right sides and diagonal lines, pin binding ends together at right angles (**Fig. 49**).

10. Machine stitch along diagonal line (**Fig. 50**), removing pins as you stitch.

11. Lay binding against quilt to double check that it is correct length.

12. Trim binding ends, leaving 1/4" seam allowance; press seam open. Stitch binding to quilt.

13. If using 2 1/2"w binding (finished size 1/2"), trim backing and batting a scant 1/4" larger than quilt top so that batting and backing will fill the binding when it is folded over to quilt backing. If using narrower binding, trim backing and batting even with edges of quilt top.

14. On one edge of quilt, fold binding over to quilt backing and pin pressed edge in place, covering stitching line (**Fig. 51**). On adjacent side, fold binding over, forming a mitered corner (**Fig. 52**). Repeat to pin remainder of binding in place.

15. Blindstitch binding to backing, taking care not to stitch through to front of quilt.

ATTACHING BINDING WITH OVERLAPPED CORNERS

1. Matching raw edges and using 1/4" seam allowance, sew a length of binding to top and bottom edges on right side of quilt.

2. If using 2 1/2"w binding (finished size 1/2"), trim backing and batting from top and bottom edges a scant 1/4" larger than quilt top so that batting and backing will fill the binding when it is folded over to quilt backing. If using narrower binding, trim backing and batting even with edges of quilt top. **Note:** For Springtime Baby quilt, trim backing and batting approximately 7/8" larger than quilt top so that batting and backing will fill the binding when it is folded over to quilt backing.

3. Trim ends of top and bottom binding even with edges of quilt top. Fold binding over to quilt backing and pin pressed edges in place, covering stitching line (**Fig. 53**); blindstitch binding to backing.

4. Leaving approximately 1 1/2" of binding at each end, stitch a length of binding to each side edge of quilt. Trim backing and batting as in Step 2.

5. Trim each end of binding 1/2" longer than bound edge. Fold each end of binding over to quilt backing (**Fig. 54**); pin in place. Fold binding over to quilt backing and blindstitch in place, taking care not to stitch through to front of quilt.

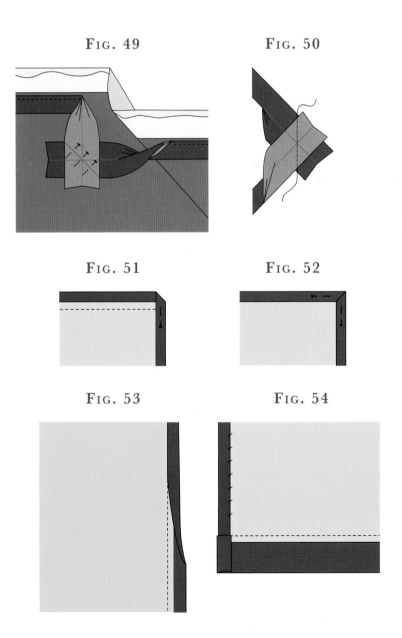

FIG. 49   FIG. 50

FIG. 51   FIG. 52

FIG. 53   FIG. 54

Pillow Finishing

If desired, you may add welting and/or a ruffle to the pillow top before sewing the pillow top and back together.

ADDING WELTING TO PILLOW TOP

1. To make welting, use bias strip indicated in project instructions. (Or measure edges of pillow top and add 4". Measure circumference of cord and add 2". Cut a bias strip of fabric the determined measurement, piecing if necessary.)
2. Lay cord along center of bias strip on wrong side of fabric; fold strip over cord. Using a zipper foot, machine baste along length of strip close to cord. Trim seam allowance to width you will use to sew pillow top and back together (see Step 2 of **Making A Knife-Edge Pillow**).
3. Matching raw edges and beginning and ending 3" from ends of welting, baste welting to right side of pillow top. To make turning corners easier, clip seam allowance of welting at pillow top corners.
4. Remove approximately 3" of seam at 1 end of welting; fold fabric away from cord. Trim remaining end of welting so that cord ends meet exactly (**Fig. 55**).

5. Fold short edge of welting fabric 1/2" to wrong side; fold fabric back over area where ends meet (**Fig. 56**).
6. Baste remainder of welting to pillow top close to cord (**Fig. 57**).
7. Follow **Making A Knife-Edge Pillow** to complete pillow.

ADDING A RUFFLE TO PILLOW TOP

1. To form ruffle, fold along length with wrong sides together and raw edges matching; press. Baste raw edges of ruffle together 1/4" from edges.
2. To gather ruffle, place quilting thread or dental floss 1/4" from raw edge of ruffle. Using a medium-width zigzag stitch with a medium stitch length, stitch over quilting thread or dental floss, being careful not to catch thread or floss in stitching. Pull quilting thread or dental floss, drawing up gathers to fit pillow top.
3. Matching raw edges, baste ruffle to right side of pillow top.
4. Follow **Making A Knife-Edge Pillow** to complete pillow.

FIG. 55   FIG. 56   FIG. 57

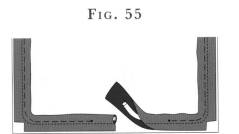 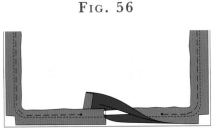 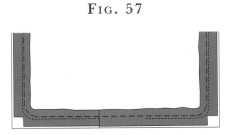

Making A Knife-Edge Pillow

1. For pillow back, cut a piece of fabric the same size as pillow top.
2. Place pillow back and pillow top right sides together. The seam allowance width you use will depend on the construction of the pillow top. If the pillow top has borders on which the finished width of the border is not crucial, use a $1/2$" seam allowance for durability. If the pillow top is pieced so that a wider seam allowance would interfere with the design, use a $1/4$" seam allowance. Using the determined seam allowance (or stitching as close as possible to welting), sew pillow top and back together, leaving an opening at bottom edge for turning.
3. Turn pillow right side out, carefully pushing corners outward. Stuff with polyester fiberfill or pillow form and sew final closure by hand.

Stenciling

1. To make stencil, use a permanent marker to trace pattern onto plastic template material; cut out design with craft knife.
2. Place stencil in position on right side of fabric. Dip brush in paint and remove excess on paper towel. Brush should be almost dry. Apply paint in a stamping motion to fill in design area. Carefully remove stencil and allow to dry. Reposition stencil as necessary to complete stenciling.

Signing And Dating Your Quilt

A completed quilt is a work of art and should be signed and dated. There are many different ways to do this and numerous books on the subject. The label should reflect the style of the quilt, the occasion or person for which it was made, and the quilter's own particular talents. Following are suggestions for recording the history of the quilt or adding a sentiment for future generations.

- Embroider quilter's name, date, and any additional information on quilt top or backing. Matching floss, such as cream floss on white border, will leave a subtle record. Bright or contrasting floss will make the information stand out.

- Make label from muslin and use permanent marker to write information. Use different colored permanent markers to make label more decorative. Stitch label to back of quilt.

- Use photo-transfer paper to add image to white or cream fabric label. Stitch label to back of quilt.

- Piece an extra block from quilt top pattern to use as label. Add information with permanent fabric pen. Appliqué block to back of quilt.

- Write message on appliquéd design from quilt top. Attach appliqué to back of the quilt.

Hand Stitches

BLANKET STITCH

Come up at 1, go down at 2, and come up at 3, keeping thread below point of needle (**Fig. 58**).

BLIND STITCH

Come up at 1, go down at 2, and come up at 3 (**Fig. 59**). Length of stitches may be varied as desired.

SATIN STITCH

Come up at 1, go down at 2, and come up at 3. Continue until area is filled (**Fig. 60**). Work stitches close together, but not overlapping.

STEM STITCH

Come up at 1. Keeping thread below the stitching line, go down at 2 and come up at 3 (**Fig. 61**).

STRAIGHT STITCH

Come up at 1 and go down at 2 (**Fig. 62**). Length of stitches may be varied as desired.

FIG. 58

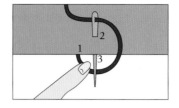

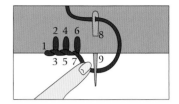

FIG. 59   **FIG. 60**

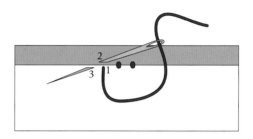

FIG. 61   **FIG. 62**

Metric Conversion Chart	
Inches x 2.54 = centimeters (cm)	Yards x .9144 = meters (m)
Inches x 25.4 = millimeters (mm)	Yards x 91.44 = centimeters (cm)
Inches x .0254 = meters (m)	Centimeters x .3937 = inches (")
	Meters x 1.0936 = yards (yd)

Standard Equivalents

⅛"	3.2 mm	0.32 cm	⅛ yard	11.43 cm	0.11 m
¼"	6.35 mm	0.635 cm	¼ yard	22.86 cm	0.23 m
⅜"	9.5 mm	0.95 cm	⅜ yard	34.29 cm	0.34 m
½"	12.7 mm	1.27 cm	½ yard	45.72 cm	0.46 m
⅝"	15.9 mm	1.59 cm	⅝ yard	57.15 cm	0.57 m
¾"	19.1 mm	1.91 cm	¾ yard	68.58 cm	0.69 m
⅞"	22.2 mm	2.22 cm	⅞ yard	80 cm	0.8 m
1"	25.4 mm	2.54 cm	1 yard	91.44 cm	0.91 m